THE OFFICIAL HISTORY OF THE TOUR de france™

Published in 2021 by Welbeck

An Imprint of Welbeck Non-Fiction Limited, part of Welbeck Publishing Group.

20 Mortimer Street London W1T 3JW

Text © Welbeck Non-Fiction Limited, part of Welbeck Publishing Group.

Tour de France trademark copyright © ASO/STF

First published by as *Le Tour de France: The Official Treasures* Carlton Books in 2007

A CIP catalogue record for this book is available from the British Library

ISBN 978-1-78739-668-5

Project Editor: Ross Hamilton
Design: Luke Griffin & Eliana Holder
Picture Research: Paul Langan
Production: Rachel Burgess

Printed in Dubai

10 9 8 7 6 5 4 3 2 1

THE OFFICIAL HISTORY OF THE

TOUR de France™

Foreword by **Bernard Hinault**, five times Tour champion

Luke Edwardes-Evans • Serge Laget • Andy McGrath

WELBECK

Contents

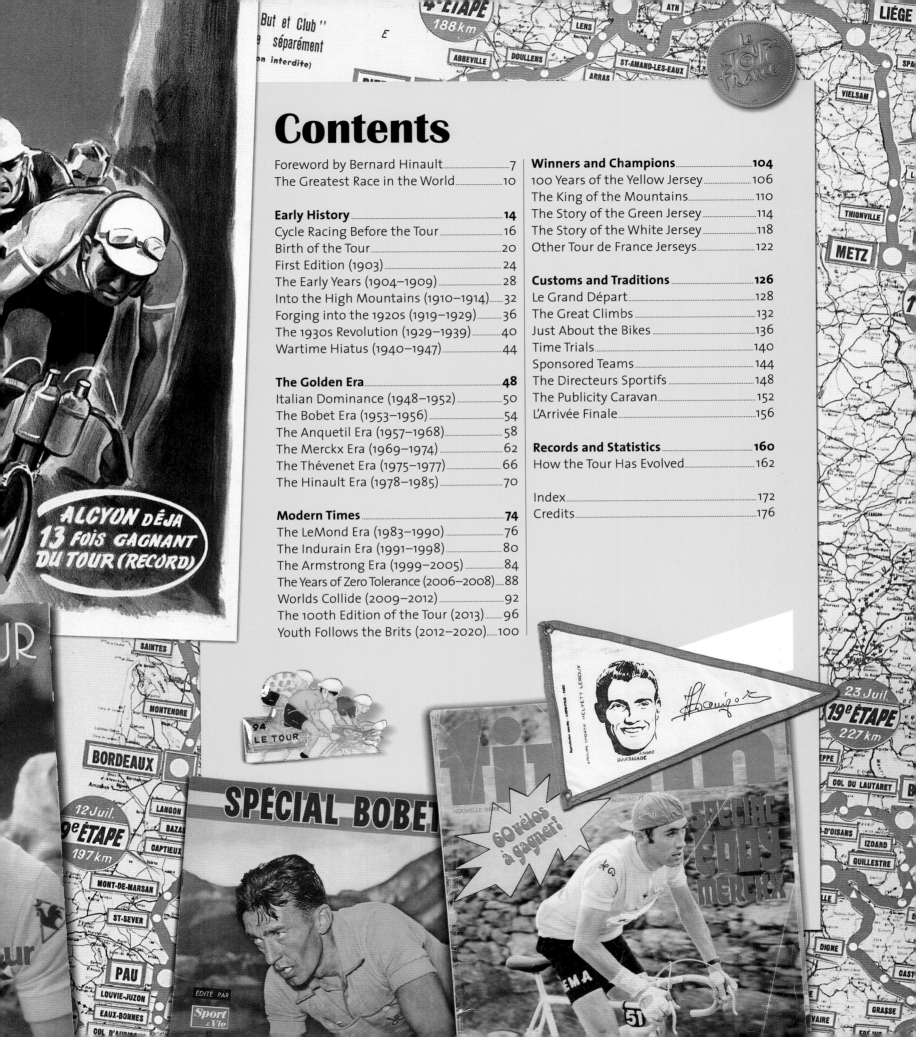

Foreword by Bernard Hinault

I have a special relationship with the Tour de France. As a teenager growing up, I watched it go by and I dreamed of racing it. Then my life was changed by it and my five successes there. I remain the last Frenchman to have won it.

What started with an idea of Henri Desgrange and 60 cyclists rolling out at dawn in 1903, is now a giant which celebrated its 100th edition in 2013. It dwarfs cycling's other races in size, prestige, scope and worldwide reach. Around the world 180 nations tune in every summer, enraptured, to see their heroes compete for glory.

Every Tour de France creates new heroes and writes a new chapter too and the finest feats and legendary stories of the Tour are recounted in these pages: Eugène Christophe forging new forks in 1913, Fausto Coppi's emphatic escapes to victory in 1949, the impudent control of Jacques Anquetil quickly succeeded by the irresistible dominance of Eddy Merckx and, later, that silent force, Miguel Indurain.

The Tour rewards a little madness, both as a cyclist suffering on the roads and an onlooker surveying the spectacle. And what a spectacle it is: from the light, loud publicity caravan to the main show, that bunch of cyclists flying by, it's one of life's extraordinary sensory experiences. Travelling through town after town as if passing on a secret, the Tour has become a part of the fabric of French life and international sport. If it's a folly, then it is a beautiful one.

The triumphs and near misses of the show perennially play out on the Tour's spectacular and ever-changing canvas. Every July, there are new places to visit, but always accompanied by the peerless spires of the Alps and Pyrenees, the rolling hills of the south and miles of sunflower fields.

The Tour de France was invented by Man, and we must remember that it is sustained by the roster of champions and the annual dramas and dénouements that help to keep us in the Tour's thrall.

Happy reading!

Bernard Hinault

LEFT: Bernard Hinault's Tour triumphs in 1978, 1979, 1981, 1982 and 1985 make him one of the event's truly legendary figures.

RIGHT: During his time as ambassador, one of Hinault's roles was to appear at stage finishes to greet stage winners and jersey holders.

The Greatest Race in the World

The Tour de France started out as a publicity stunt designed to shore up indifferent sales of a sports newspaper. A century later the Tour is a worldwide phenomenon and an icon of French life.

It's come a long way since the first edition in 1903, and the modern version is a global event with an audience of millions, but the Tour is essentially the same beautiful, brutal and often quite baffling three-week race. To the professional cyclist it remains the ultimate challenge in terms of physical endurance, danger and earning power. To the roadside fan it's a noisy carnival, with 200 cyclists flashing by somewhere in between. It works on every level and that is at the heart of the Tour's appeal.

Live colour television has transformed the Tour de France into a race of beauty unparallelled in sport. Since the advent of live coverage in 1972 the mesmerising pattern of a peloton flowing along the roads of France has opened up the Tour to a whole new audience who can enjoy the race from the perspective of a lofty bystander, rejoicing in the images, without having to take any great interest in the minutiae of the contest.

A bicycle race can be enjoyed either superficially or in fine detail. The bike fanatic can watch hours of live television coverage, and read every day about the outcome of each stage on the internet and in the papers, most notably *L'Equipe*, the sports newspaper whose ancestry goes all the way back to *L'Auto* – the organising newspaper which created the Tour at the start of the last century. With 20 stages and a prologue, nearly 200 riders, and three weeks of unfolding competition, there is never enough space or time to relate the thousands of incidents and human interest stories that occur during the Tour de France.

MYTH AND MAYHEM

Any modern sports promoter would normally avoid the sort of unpredictable events that can happen outside the controlled environment of a stadium or racetrack. The Tour doesn't make

PREVIOUS PAGES: The best Grand Départ in Tour history? In 2014 the 101st edition started with two stages in Yorkshire and a third which travelled south to London. Huge, enthusiastic crowds cheered the race through many traditional Yorkshire towns.

LEFT: Epic mountain stages in the early 1900s made heroes out of the riders and created many of the legendary stories that established the Tour as the ultimate cycling challenge.

ABOVE: Goggles and leather face mask as worn by a Tour follower from the early years when rough roads threw up clouds of dust wherever the peloton went.

any sense; it's a crazy race, the product of a bygone age when the bicycle rivalled anything on road and track and was used to test the heroic endurance of the best athletes of the day. In fact, modern Tours bear little resemblance to the pre-war Tours and those of the 1920s, when riders walked alone up unmade mountain passes and had to repair their own machines without assistance of any kind.

How many spectators were watching when in the 1913 Tour Eugène Christophe banged in desperation on the door of the village forge in Ste Marie-de-Campan and begged the blacksmith to lend him his tools so that he could repair his fork after breaking it on the rough roads in the Pyrenees? Very few, surely, apart from the race judges who ensured that he

worked unaided, and the boy who worked the bellows – earning Christophe a three-minute penalty to add to the two hours already lost in the forge. This is one of the many legends of the Tour that were witnessed by no more than a few bystanders. Part true story, part myth, the history of the Tour de France is an elaborate construction, relying on the veracity – or lack of it – of colourful accounts by reporters caught up in the infectious drama of the race.

BELOW: Modern Tours attract roadside fans in their millions. Mountain stages are always the most heavily supported.

BOTTOM: The Tour is more than 100 years old – the cars following belong in museums and the bikes were crude and heavy and frequently broke down or punctured.

THE GREATEST RACE IN THE WORLD

11

TOP: After three weeks of racing, the Champs-Elysées in the heart of Paris is the traditional finale of the Tour.

BOTTOM: Yellow is the leader's colour including this yellow cap – a Tour innovation which has been copied many times by other stage races around the world.

RIGHT: The polka dot jersey is awarded to the best climber in the Tour and, like the other coloured jerseys, is highly prized.

OPPOSITE TOP: The Tour has transcended sport to become a French cultural staple. People come out in droves in route-side towns to see the race pass and cheer on their favourite riders.

OPPOSITE BOTTOM: Arnaud Démare celebrates a hard-found victory at Stage 18 of the 2018 Tour de France.

UNIQUE EXPERIENCE

What the newspapers, television and radio can never show, however, is the unique experience of the one roadside Tour fan who may have glimpsed Christophe in the forge, or any of the many bizarre incidents that have occurred on every stage of the Tour since its inception. That is where the power of the race lies, in its accessibility to the public at stage towns and on the open road, its unpredictability, and of course the simple fact that it is a free show.

In this book we have divided the Tour into its most significant eras, relating some of the epic stories and giving a flavour of the overall race. There are also chapters which look at the history and development of specific aspects of the Tour, ranging from the famous coloured jerseys to the evolution of the racing bike. Meanwhile, superb images of Tour treasures, selected from the peerless collection of memorabilia collected by Serge Laget at the Société du Tour de France and presented here in all their glory, convey the authentic feel of each successive era.

As a sporting occasion the Tour is in a class of its own, and the rich and varied history of the race, its highs and lows, could fill these pages many times over. Now well beyond its 100th edition in 2013, the Tour has weathered the dark aftermath of the Armstrong era and has enjoyed a much healthier image in recent times thanks to better testing protocols and cleaner ethical practices among teams of the World Tour.

What started out as little more than a publicity stunt, witnessed here and there by amazed onlookers, is now broadcast to more than one billion viewers across 190 countries around the world.

Roadside fans alone are estimated at 12 million. Thanks to incredible aerial imagery and on-bike cameras, the internet and social media, the Tour de France has broadened its appeal and is now reaching a younger generation of fans.

Owners Amaury Sport Organisation (ASO) have secured the future of the Tour as one of the premier global sporting events. They have safeguarded its future financially without losing its status as a French national treasure. As an advertisement for one of the world's most beautiful countries, nothing beats the Tour's three-week odyssey. And, for cycling fans, the Tour de France remains the ultimate gladiatorial clash of the champions in the home of cycling.

Early History

A stunt dreamed up by newspapermen, the first Tour de France saw a rag-tag bunch of cyclists waved off from outside a bar on the outskirts of Paris in 1903. Rapidly the Tour expanded into a race with legendary champions, a set of iconic leader's jerseys and a wanderlust that took the race into the farthest corners of France. Mountains have become mythical and tales of Tour intrigue, nuance and controversy abound – and the Tour continued to grow, along with its history, folklore and following.

LEFT: No plastic bottles in those days. The bunch in the 1923 race take a drinks break.

Cycle Racing Before the Tour

Bicycle racing in France was a hugely popular sport long before the outlandish notion of a Tour de France was dreamed up in 1902.

France is credited as the country in which the first recorded bicycle race was held, on 31 May 1868 in the Parc de St Cloud in Paris. Seven riders, all of them sitting astride a revolutionary new machine, made such an impression on those present that a whole series of events sprang up to cater for a rapidly growing sport. It could hardly fail, as the sight of swashbuckling athletes riding wheel to wheel had all the elements of great sporting spectacle – speed, danger and fascinating machines.

BIRTH OF CYCLE RACING

A two-wheeler with pedals fixed to the front hoop cranked around by a rider was the brainchild of French coachmaker Pierre Michaux in 1867. The bigger the wheel, the more ground could be covered with each revolution. At a pedal stroke, literally, the era of the Draisienne or Hobby Horse, propelled by rhythmic paddling on the ground either side of a wheeled frame, was ended, and the *Velocipède à pédale* became an instant hit. By 1869 there were 60 makers of these fashionable machines in Paris and a further 15 beyond the capital. France led the way both in terms of the

conception and production of the new bicycle, and also in the promotion of bicycle racing.

Britain would later catch up in the race to create bicycles both for leisure use and racing, but during this period machines from France were the choice of serious riders. One, James Moore, a vet living in Paris, won the first Paris–Rouen race, held in November 1869. His average speed for the 123km was an impressive 11.8kph, or 7.5mph, which included stops and was achieved over rough roads in wet weather. Moore's bike was French-built with metal, not wooden, spokes and rims, and tyres made from solid rubber. In the hubs were steel ball bearings, polished by the inmates of the St Pelagie prison. The prison governor made Moore's innovative bicycle, which was one of the first racing machines and weighed 25kg. The Franco-Prussian war in 1870–71 put the burgeoning French bicycle industry on hold, and across the Channel the British seized the opportunity to lead the way by developing the high-wheeled Ordinary, or Penny Farthing, and later the Safety bicycle, while

BELOW: Track events were hugely popular at the turn of the century.

EARLY HISTORY

16

Pierre Giffard

Pierre Giffard organised, in 1891, the first Paris–Brest–Paris and Bordeaux–Paris races, and was editor of *Le Vélo*, a cycling paper founded in 1892 which soon sold 80,000 copies daily. Giffard was a cycling evangelist who, writing in *Le Petit Journal* and *Le Figaro* in 1890, predicted a great future for cycling. As editor of *Le Vélo*, he promoted cycle races to boost sales of the paper and it was only when he wrote an article in defence of Alfred Dreyfus, a Jewish French army officer charged with spying, that his anti-Dreyfus backers took their money elsewhere and started *L'Auto-Vélo*, in direct opposition to *Le Vélo* and with Henri Desgrange as editor. Giffard lost the circulation battle with Desgrange. In 1904 *Le Vélo* closed and Giffard was declared bankrupt. He briefly worked as a reporter for *L'Auto* and died in 1923.

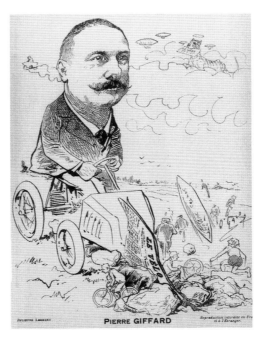

TOP LEFT: Major Taylor, one of the first black sports stars, was widely acclaimed when he came over from the USA to race in Europe in the early 1900s.

FAR LEFT: A warmly dressed early motorist reads a copy of Henri Desgrange's *L'Auto-Vélo*, later changed to just *L'Auto*.

LEFT: A caricature of Henri Desgrange's rival Pierre Giffard shows him running his own publication, *Le Vélo*, into the ground.

BOTTOM LEFT: Media accreditation for Alphonse Steines, editor of *L'Auto-Vélo*, for 1900.

"The two-wheeled velocipede is the animal which will supersede everything else."

THE VELOCIPEDIST, 1869

also popularising racing and record-breaking on cinder tracks. Through the 1870s and 80s, the British and once again the French cycling scene poured their ingenuity into the chain-driven Safety bicycle, while racing events grew in length on both road and track. In the final decade of the nineteenth century the bicycle, pretty much as we know it today, was a hugely popular vehicle, used for both transport and competition. Long-distance marathon races in 1891 from Paris to Brest and back (1,200km), and from Bordeaux to Paris (572km) were astonishing demonstrations of the efficiency of the bike. Average speed for the winner of the Bordeaux–Paris race was 13.5mph (21.7kmh).

Every type of racing was tried out in the 1890s, from 24-hour endurance track races to sprint events and long-distance road trials with individual riders paced by multiple tandem crews or early versions of the motor car. In the USA, marathon track events often held over six days pitted teams against each other over incredible distances exceeding 4,000km (2,500 miles). These events were held at the Madison Square Gardens track in New York and are still known as Madison races or *races à l'américain* in France.

SOLITARY TESTS

Road racing during this period was very much a solo challenge, with riders either paced on the road or riding alone with no assistance from a bunch, or peloton. That was the ideal of a 27-year-old Parisian called Henri Desgrange, who on 11 May 1893 became the first holder of the hour record, riding 35.325km, or 21.9 miles, on the Buffalo track in Paris. Ten years later the same Desgrange, by then director of the sports paper *L'Auto*, would promote a stunt that combined the long-distance place-to-place road trials with the formula of a six-stage race that mirrored the track Madison Sixes from the USA. The Tour de France for bicycles would be a first, and the sport of cycling would never be the same again.

Charles Terront

Michelin's Charles Terront was the first winner of the Paris–Brest–Paris in 1891. His time for the 1,198km marathon was 71-37, nine hours ahead of Jiel-Laval, riding for Dunlop, in second place. At 1,200km, the "P–B–P" is the oldest racing event that is still regularly run, although these days it is a "sportive" event held once every four years. Terront was born in 1857 in St Ouen and was a professional cyclist from 1875 to 1894. He rode during the era of the Ordinary and the Safety bicycles and had a formidable reputation over long distances, winning six-day track events and road marathons in Europe and the USA. In 1893 he set a record for the ride from St Petersburg to Paris, covering 2,836km in 14 days and seven hours.

BELOW Booklet showing the range of bicycles produced by La Française, which supplied machines to the first Tour winner, Maurice Garin.

OPPOSITE: Charles Terront (right), the winner of the first ever Paris–Brest–Paris race, holds a competitor's bike at the 1910 Tour.

LEFT: The French cyclist Charles Terront, who won the first Paris–Brest–Paris cycle race, September 1891.

LEFT: Maurice Garin is pictured on the cover of *Le Petit Journal* winning the Paris to Brest road race in 1901.

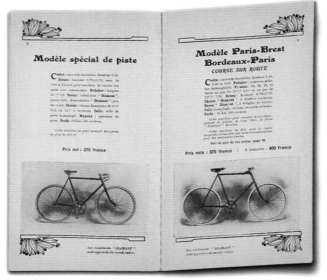

Birth of the Tour

As a marketing gimmick the Tour de France took some beating. Henri Desgrange may not have had the original idea, but his careful handling of the nascent concept ensured its survival.

A working lunch: what better way to combine a spot of business, some gossip and a few pie-in-the-sky ideas than across a white linen tablecloth, a couple of bottles of wine and the plat du jour? If you had walked into the Zimmer Madrid restaurant on Boulevard Montmartre in Paris on 20 November 1902, the animated conversation from a table with three men would not have aroused undue attention. Soberly dressed in black frock coats with waistcoats and starched collars, they looked no different from the businessmen at the other tables taking a traditional long French lunch.

There's more to this group than meets the eye, however. The discussion is animated, mainly serious but punctuated by laughter, some of it incredulous. One moment of uproar is particularly noticeable. Diners in the restaurant momentarily put down their spoons of onion soup to see what the fuss is about. One of our group has just come up with an idea that is quite frankly preposterous to at least one of the others. The man who has their attention is Geo Lefèvre, a writer on the sports newspaper *L'Auto-Vélo*.

He has an idea for what we would today call a marketing promotion, but such an anodyne phrase could never do justice to Lefèvre's crackpot notion of a bicycle race around the whole of France, to be completed in just six marathon stages. Such a stunt, he says, would generate pages of colourful stories that would capture the imagination of the French public. More to the point, sales of *L'Auto-Vélo* would take off, and their great rival, *Le Vélo*, would suffer.

DUELLING NEWSPAPERS

With this Lefèvre had the attention of his *L'Auto-Vélo* colleagues. The paper's accountant, Victor Goddet, perhaps surprisingly, reacted with enthusiasm. His editor, a former champion bike racer turned journalist, was more measured in his reaction. Henri Desgrange knew who would carry the responsibility for an event with such massive publicity potential. Of the three men sitting at that dining table on a nondescript November lunchtime, it was he who understood the enormity of the undertaking, the consequences of failure and also, quite probably, the brilliance of an idea of truly historic proportions.

ABOVE: Front cover of *L'Auto* showing results from the scandal-hit second Tour in 1904.

RIGHT: Desgrange (centre) with 1932 Tour de France winner André Leducq of France.

"I have dreamed many sporting dreams but never have I conceived of anything as worthy as this reality."

HENRI DESGRANGE (1903)

COMŒDIA

ABONNEMENTS :

Journal Quotidien illustré à 4, 6 et 8 pages

Rédacteur en chef: G. DE PAWLOWSKI

Le Numéro : 5 centimes

Paris le 23/I 1908

Monsieur Pierre Lafitte
E.V.

Mon cher ami,
Je t'adresse sous ce pli et le projet de regle ment que m' a fait remettre avant son départ pour Montpellier ton rédacteur en chef et le reglement que j'ai fait moi-même

1o J'ai fixé la date de la seconde éliminatoire au Dimanche 23 Février,mais je n'ai pas besoin de te dire que je ne tiens à cette date que si elle te convient

2o Je t'ai laissé le soin de fixer la date de La Eliminatoire finale.

3o Je n'ai pas indiqué de secondes Eliminatoires en province parce que cela m'a semblé tout au moins inutile, surtout en présence des billets de chemin de fer qu'il va falloir trouver pour tous ces lapins là

4o J'ai imposé aux concurrents de la seconde éliminatoire l'obligation de se faire entendre aupara vant soit à Comoedia soit à Musica:j'ai eu peur en effet d'après la cinquantaine de lettres que j'ai reçues que nous ne soyions inondés de candidats et qu'une soirée entière n'y suffise pas.Nous éviterons aussi des inscriptions de farceurs.Si ces auditions préalables à Comoedia t'embetent,tu n'as qu'à enle ver dans le reglement la faculté pour eux d'aller au ditionner préalablement à Musica:ils n'auront qu'à venir tous à Comoedia

5o Enfin,tu reconnaitras ma générosité proverbia le dans les deux faits suivants:A: je laisse aux ré gionaux le soin de nantir de passes les ténors qu'ils nous enverront à Paris.Du reste,je serais hors d'état à Comoedia qui est dans sa première année d'obtenir sur les Chemins de fer le moindre permis

B Je n'indique rien pour le paiement des frais de séjour à Paris.N'estimes-tu pas avec moi que le fait et l'honneur de participer à un concours sembla ble doit impliquer pour les concurrents un petit sa-

COMPTE-RENDU QUOTIDIEN
des théâtres subventionnés

LES LETTRES DE L'OUVREUSE
TOUS LES LUNDIS

Publication de Nouveautés musicales

21

BIRTH OF THE TOUR

TOP RIGHT: Letter from Henri Desgrange about the arrangements for the Tour and the number of expected entrants.

ABOVE: Henri Desgrange, the Father of the Tour, by Raoul Cabrol in 1932.

RIGHT: Henri Desgrange, pictured in 1903.

Henri Desgrange

Paris-born Henri Desgrange was a legal clerk when he took up cycling. He was a talented rider and in 1893, aged 28, set the first hour record, covering 35.326km (21.9 miles) in one hour on the Buffalo track of a Paris suburb. He became a journalist, but an unexpected event landed him at the head of a new sports paper, L'Auto-Vélo, in 1900. Pierre Giffard had founded Le Vélo in 1892, but the idealistic Giffard was enraged at the treatment of French army officer Albert Dreyfus, a Jew falsely accused of spying for Germany, and lobbied for him in Le Vélo. Among the anti-Dreyfus brigade, however, were a number of Le Vélo's financial backers. They decided to abandon Le Vélo and start a new paper, Le Vélo-Auto, with Desgrange as its director.

L'Equipe

Since 1946 *L'Equipe* has been the successor to *L'Auto*, the paper run by Henri Desgrange which profited handsomely from the first Tour in 1903. Motorsport, however, was the inspiration for the paper's title. *L'Auto*'s great rivalry with *Le Vélo* was short-lived. On changing its name in 1903 from *L'Auto-Vélo* to *L'Auto* the launch of the Tour de France in July was an overnight success for the re-branded paper. Circulation more than doubled to 60,000, and by 1908 it was 250,000. It reached a peak of 854,000 in 1933 under Desgrange. *Le Vélo* changed its name in 1904 to *Le Journal de l'Automobile* and never troubled *L'Auto* again. Today *L'Equipe* is France's number-one daily paper, with regular sales exceeding 300,000. It honours *L'Auto* in its motor racing section where the title is still printed in the same gothic typescript of the original.

RIGHT: A *L'Equipe* front page from the 1953 Tour proclaims Louison Bobet's brilliance after claiming the yellow jersey on the stage between Gap and Briançon.

Desgrange was right to be cautious. He was locked in a circulation battle with rival sport paper *Le Vélo*, and both titles were languishing with sales around 25,000. The rivalry was more than commercial, however. It dated back to 1900, when a split between the editor of *Le Vélo*, Pierre Giffard, and its backers led to the founding of a new rival paper. In 1900 *L'Auto-Vélo* was launched with support from the old *Le Vélo* backers Michelin, Clement and De Dion. At the editorial helm was Desgrange, with Goddet keeping the books. *Le Vélo* was printed on green paper; *L'Auto-Vélo* countered with yellow.

BRINGING AN IDEA TO REALITY

Promoting bike races was an integral part of running the paper, generating sales from the stories of the riders and the races. Desgrange was immediately successful, organising the second edition of Paris–Brest as well as the first Marseilles–Paris and Bordeaux–Paris – all marathon challenges contested by the leading riders of the time. So when Goddet suggested stringing together a nationwide tour comprising six such marathons with rest days in between, Desgrange grasped the appeal immediately, but he sucked his teeth at the thought of pulling it all together.

It had to happen though – a "Tour de France" for bicycles was too good an idea to leave to others. On 19 January 1903, just two months after that fateful working lunch at the Zimmer Madrid, *L'Auto* (Giffard had by now taken legal action to prevent them from using "Le Vélo" in the paper's title) announced on its front page a new event to take place later the same year: "The Tour de France, the greatest cycle race in the world". At that point the Tour was still just an idea – Desgrange had yet to contract any riders, and the route was little more than a few towns scribbled on a napkin.

Desgrange was right to be daunted. By April he had only 15 riders contracted to appear in his publicity stunt, which at least had a route worked out and running dates 31 May to 5 July. The six stages were also set, to run between Paris, Lyons, Marseilles, Toulouse, Bordeaux, Nantes and Paris. Desgrange moved the date back from 1 July to 18 July, halved the length of the stages and reduced the entrance fee. It worked: by the end of June there were 78 entrants, a race route, and prize money. The first Tour de France was about to begin.

RIGHT: Tour winner Gino Bartali and his Italian team ride a lap of honour at the Parc des Princes at the end of the 1938 Tour.

OPPOSITE PAGE: Jacques Goddet (in white) talks to Antonin Magne in 1934.

23

BIRTH OF THE TOUR

First Edition (1903)

Six mammoth stages awaited the group of hardened professionals, adventurers and chancers who came together on the start line of the first Tour on 1 July 1903.

Road works outside the Reveil-Matin bar in Montgeron on the outskirts of Paris forced the organisers to move the start of the first Tour de France a little way down the road, where 60 cyclists were sent off on a journey into the unknown. Nineteen days later, back in the capital, 21 survivors were cheered to the rooftops as they paraded around the Parc des Princes track. Of the non-finishers at the end of the six-stage, 2,426km race, many had been ejected for cheating, some had abandoned through fatigue and injury, and a few simply disappeared.

The six stages, which married the popular format of a six-day track event with the romance of long-distance, place-to-place, unpaced road races, went from Paris to Lyons, Lyons to Marseilles, Marseilles to Toulouse, Toulouse to Bordeaux, Bordeaux to Nantes and Nantes to Paris. All were individual, non-stop stages, but there were seven days of rest to allow the battered and dust-encrusted warriors a fleeting chance to recover. There were no transfers between stages, and by keeping the loop south of Paris and inside the great mountain ranges of the Alps and Pyrenees the first Tour was more than 1,000km shorter than modern Tours. Factor in the terrible roads – choking with dust in the dry, and slippery with mud in the wet – unreliable and heavy bikes and the solo nature of the contest, and the organiser pitched it just right.

DAZZLING DEBUT

The first edition of the Tour de France was a runaway success, inspiring massive interest from the French public and galloping sales of *L'Auto*, which printed endless pages devoted to the event in special editions. Tour founder and director of *L'Auto* Henri Desgrange had failed to achieve his dream of creating a race so gruelling that only one man would finish, but got pretty close, and a great sporting event was born.

"And that was the first Tour de France! I wish the hours of work and great satisfaction the race has meant for us could go on indefinitely."

HENRI DESGRANGE, 1903

TOP: Maurice Garin, the first champion of the Tour, prepares for the victory parade at the Parc des Princes in Paris. Garin Jnr is also suitably equipped for the occasion.

RIGHT: Au Reveil-Matin, the bar on the outskirts of Paris, where the Tour legend was finally made real.

ABOVE LEFT: Charles Laeser of Switzerland won the stage and thus became the first non-French rider to win a Tour de France stage.

ABOVE RIGHT: A real pioneer of early professional cycling, Maurice Garin, winner of the first Tour, pictured in 1902.

TOP: Competitors in the general classification competition reach the end of the stage.

Maurice Garin

A professional cyclist riding for the La Française team was the winner of the first Tour. Maurice Garin, a Frenchman with Italian parents from the northern mining town of Lens, had won the Paris–Roubaix in 1897–98, the 1,200km Paris–Brest–Paris in 1901 and the 1902 Bordeaux–Paris marathon in 1902. Nicknamed "The Little Chimney Sweep" and "The White Bulldog" owing to his habit of riding in a white jacket, Garin was a long-distance champion who also held the paced record for 500km of 15-02-32 set in 1895 and was the winner of numerous place-to-place races across France in the 1890s. Garin quit racing after he was disqualified from first place in the 1904 Tour. He made a comeback and finished the race in 1911 before retiring for good and running a garage in Lens. He died aged 86 in 1957.

26

ABOVE: Riders prepare to leave the Nantes velodrome before the final stage of the Tour.

LEFT: Garin is clearly visible in his trademark white jacket as he rounds a bend in the centre of the pack during the 1903 race.

Le Tour de France

Stage one started at 3.16pm and headed south-east from Paris to Lyons. At 467km it was the second longest stage of the remaining five and France's Maurice Garin was first across the cobbles into Lyons at nine o'clock the following morning. Less than a minute behind, Hippolyte Pagie, riding for Cycles Pagie of Tourcoing, was close on Garin's heels and had the reporters licking their lips at the prospect of a close contest. Pagie would abandon the race later, however, leaving second place to Garin's team-mate Lucien Pothier, whose best place was third on stage five from Bordeaux to Nantes (425km), won by Garin in 27-47-00.

Garin also won the final stage, the longest of the race from Nantes back to Paris (471km), to record three stage wins and a convincing overall victory. Other stages were won by Hippolyte Aucouturier, who abandoned the race on stage one with stomach cramps having drunk copious amounts of red wine, but won stages two and three as an unclassified rider. Stage four was taken by the first non-French stage winner in the Tour, Charles Laeser of Switzerland, who failed to finish in either of the first two years.

A NATION INSPIRED

Stage starts were not always designed with spectators in mind. Two were flagged away last thing at night, and one before dawn. All the stages took at least 24 hours to complete, and riders were expected to feed themselves and make repairs to their bicycles without outside assistance.

After a total riding time of 94-33-14 Garin finished 2-59-02 ahead of Pothier, a margin between first and second overall that has never been exceeded. His average speed was 25.69kph, or nearly 16mph, some 10mph slower than the Tour a hundred years later. The crowds that came out in increasing numbers as the race worked its clockwise way around France were not interested in the speed of the riders so much as their heroic tales of endurance, described in the most colourful language throughout the pages of *L'Auto*. A few dozen curious onlookers had turned out on 1 July to see the Tour leave Paris. On its return on 19 July to the stage finish at Ville d'Avray, there were 100,000 in attendance, and a further 20,000 were at the Parc des Princes track for the final victory parade.

Hippolyte Aucouturier

Hippolyte Aucouturier, "Le Terrible", won two stages in the first Tour de France but could not compete for the overall prize having already abandoned the race on the first stage. The rules allowed for a rider to ride on a stage-by-stage basis, but Desgrange did not have a way to exclude him from figuring in the overall classification. He tried to handicap Aucouturier after his win on stage two, but the man from Allier caught the leaders and won stage three to Toulouse. An embarrassing situation was resolved when on stage four from Toulouse to Bordeaux a dog brought down a bunch of riders, Aucouturier among them, following which he abandoned the race for good.

LEFT: An artist's sketch of Aucouturier racing the 1903 Paris-Roubaix.

TOP LEFT: The Tour inspired books and stories that featured the race in a very romantic light.

TOP RIGHT: Onlookers witness the race as it rattles through the southern French town of Castres in a cloud of dust.

The Early Years (1904–1909)

After the stunning success of the first Tour de France in 1903, it was not unreasonable to expect even greater acclaim in the years that followed.

Tour founder Henri Desgrange and his organising team at the sports newspaper *L'Auto* had every reason to enjoy a honeymoon period after the runaway popularity of the inaugural Tour de France in 1903. It lasted a little over 12 months, till 2 July 1904, when the second Tour headed out of Paris in the direction of Lyons – and into trouble, lots of it. Things looked promising at the start, with a bigger field of 88 riders headed by 1903 winner Maurice Garin but with a strong rival in Hippolyte Aucouturier. Nor would there be any confusion over riders competing for individual stages but not the overall classification, as the rules now stated that a rider who failed to finish a stage could neither return to bag individual stages nor compete in the overall standings, as Aucouturier had done in 1903.

Garin won the first stage from Paris to Lyons (467km), but a crash for Aucouturier during the stage cast him over two hours adrift of Garin. After a five-day rest period the race continued with the second of six stages, destination Marseilles, 374km away. During the stage Garin was stopped and roughed up by a mob who favoured a regional rider, Alfred Faure. The widespread use of cars inside and outside the race also proved too tempting for some riders who "door-handled" their way to the front, and it was even alleged that some competitors took train rides to circumvent the route.

CHEATS AND CHICANERY

Partisan crowds in St Etienne and Nîmes harassed riders, blocked roads and caused havoc, strewing broken bottles and tin tacks along the route. Officials only got through after brandishing pistols at the hostile crowds. Widespread accusations of cheating were levelled at the leading riders, and when Garin arrived in Paris on 23 July as the winner once again, an announcement was soon made that the result of the race would face the equivalent

ABOVE: Henri Cornet of France was eventually declared the winner after the scandal-hit Tour of 1904, but he had to wait until December of the same year to find out.

BELOW: The 1905 Tour de France winner, Louis Trousselier, pictured during his victorious campaign.

Louis Trousselier

Louis Trousselier was one of the most popular riders of the era. He won the 1905 Tour, taking five stages on the way. As a soldier in the French army, Trousselier didn't have time to enjoy the spoils of victory. He was called back to his battalion the next day, having been given special leave by his commanding officer. The Parisian was a showman with a deft hand for bike acrobatics, able to perform nimble dismounts. Rumour has it the moustachioed Frenchman lost all his winnings from his successful Tour in a game of dice soon afterwards. Trousselier was a surer bet on the bike during his career, winning two tough one-day Classics, the 1905 Paris–Roubaix and the 1908 Bordeaux–Paris. He won four stages in the 1906 Tour and was third overall, but never returned to his previous heights.

POUR DÉVORER DES KILOMÊTRES!

il vous faut....

PARIS → 350€

LA BICYCLETTE ELIMS PIERRE

10. Faubourg Montmartre.(Cour de L'Auto.)

ABOVE: Nine riders fan across the long road from Bayonne to Bordeaux during the 1908 Tour.

LEFT: A postcard advertising the Elims Pierre Bicycle.

BELOW: Louis Trousselier is first into a corner on the Metz to Belfort stage of the 1909 Tour.

of a stewards' inquiry, carried out by the Union Vélocipédique de France. In December the verdict was issued: Garin was disqualified; Aucouturier was stripped of four stage wins; and runner-up Lucien Pothier was banned for life. All were accused of indiscretions that ranged from accepting lifts from cars to eating at the wrong time and place. The winner was a 20-year-old who had placed fifth overall, Henri Cornet.

Desgrange lamented in the pages of *L'Auto* that his beloved Tour de France was finished. "The Tour de France is over," he wrote, "and its second celebration will also, I deeply fear, be its last." As has been shown in more recent times, however, the Tour rides out scandals and chicanery that might sink lesser events. Sales of *L'Auto* remained buoyant, and after a few more rule changes and the introduction of the first big hills in the race, the 1905 Tour was presented to the public as a crusade for the reform of cycling. From 1905 to 1912 the general classification was decided by points, not by each rider's total elapsed time, and the race got longer too, with 11 stages in 1905 totalling 2,994km. Louis Trousselier rode consistently to win the 1905 race,

"Speeding over the Ballon d'Alsace is much easier for me than writing a newspaper article."

RENÉ POTTIER, 1906 TOUR WINNER

Checkpoints

In the early years of the Tour every rider's machine was stamped with a number at the start. These bikes were referred to as "Poinçonnées", meaning stamped or punched. A bicycle in the Tour de France could only be repaired, not replaced in whole or part, and they were regularly checked by race officials. At overnight stops the machines were guarded by a gendarme to prevent illicit repairs or sabotage by a rival. Machines from this era were sturdy but still prone to tube fractures caused by crashes and the constant hammering from rough and unmade roads. Punctures, whether from sabotage (tin tacks thrown in the road) or just from sharp objects, were a common occurrence and every rider carried a spare tyre wrapped around their shoulders.

benefiting from the withdrawal of René Pottier, who was first to the top of the Tour's first mountain, the Ballon d'Alsace, but fell out of the race a few days later after injuring his leg in a crash while in the lead. The race was not without trouble, however, and tin tacks on the road during the first stage from Paris to Nancy (340km) resulted in just 15 riders finishing the stage out of 60 starters. Once again the regulations were overlooked and a full field assembled for the second stage from Nancy to Besançon (299km).

THE TOUR EXPANDS

More changes and extra kilometres were piled on to the 1906 Tour. The total distance was now 4,543km, more than 2,000km longer than the first Tour and now made up of 13 stages, some of which for the first time required a transfer by car from the stage finish to the start of the next leg. This was also the year that the Tour became "La Grande Boucle" (The Great Loop), reaching out to the far corners of the French hexagon, and in 1906 going beyond – into Germany, Spain and Italy. This was also the year that the *flamme rouge*, the red kite, was flown above the road, signalling one kilometre to go to the finish. Pottier, the ace climber who once again won the stage over the Ballon d'Alsace, the Col de Laffrey and the Col Bayard, plus four others, took the overall

honours in Paris. Pottier committed suicide in January the next year, ending what could have been an illustrious Tour record.

One more stage took the total to 14 in the 1907 Tour, which visited Switzerland for the first time and added climbs of the Col de Porte and the Col de Sappey in the Chartreuse. Lucien Petit-Breton won the race, having inherited the lead from Tour favourite Louis Trousselier, who had withdrawn in protest at the penalty imposed on race leader Emile Georget for finishing stage nine from Toulouse to Bayonne (299km) on a borrowed bike.

In 1908 Petit-Breton lined up at the head of what was arguably the first super-team. Peugeot had already won the team classification of the three previous Tours and would take a fourth, plus the individual overall victory thanks to Petit-Breton, in 1908. The French bicycle manufacturer had a rider for every terrain and won all 14 stages, placing four riders in the top four overall. Petit-Breton was tactically astute and strong, riding with incredible consistency to finish in the first four in all but one stage, when he was tenth. His five stage wins resulted in a conclusive Tour double – the first rider to do so. The Tour in just its sixth year was already well on the way to becoming a regular fixture in the French summer sports and social calendar, with thousands taking time off to watch the race and many more following its progress through the pages of *L'Auto*, which by now was enjoying sales of a quarter of a million.

A giant from Luxembourg, François Faber, dominated the 1909 Tour and became the first overall winner from outside France. His all-powerful Alcyon team almost emulated the performance of Peugeot the previous year, with wins in 13 of the 14 stages, six of them by the six-foot Faber who excelled in atrocious weather that July. Many riders abandoned a race that was considered one of the hardest in Tour history as gales, snow blizzards and quagmire conditions made this a Tour of survival. Of the 150 starters only 55 made it to Paris.

LEFT: Crowds throng the road as François Faber leads the race near the end of the 1909 Caen to Paris stage.

TOP LEFT: Georges Passerieu and Albert Dupont, pictured in 1908.

OPPOSITE: François Faber of Luxembourg was a big and powerful Tour rider, winner of the Tour in 1909, and seen here running across the line at the end of the fourth stage from Belfort to Lyon.

Into the High Mountains (1910–1914)

Tours in the run-up to the First World War witnessed a decline in French domination and the advent of tremendous climbing stages through the Pyrenees and Alps.

EARLY HISTORY

32

Stages through the Pyrenees and Alps, a return to the general classification based on time and not points, and the introduction of rudimentary gear systems all helped shape the Tour in the pre-war years. The style of racing was changing too, with small groups of riders coming together in a bunch, or peloton, often resulting in sprint finishes on flatter stages. This hardly made the racing any easier – many stages were still more than 300km long and one or two each year exceeded 400km, or 250 miles. Powerful teams backed by bicycle manufacturers continued to attract the best riders, clean up many of the stages and claim top overall positions. French squads Alcyon and Peugeot also helped to introduce the first non-French winners, opening up the race to Belgian champions who would henceforth have an influence on the race out of all proportion to the size of their nation.

In 1910 the Tour entered the Pyrenees for the first time. Stage 10 was the first great mountain stage in Tour history, a 326km trek from Luchon to Bayonne over the now legendary cols of the Peyresourde, Aspin, Tourmalet and Aubisque. This and the preceding stage nine, over the Col de Porte, Portet d'Aspet and Portet des Ares, were won by French climbing ace Octave Lapize, who walked and rode his way across the summit passes, leaving the field in tatters many hours behind. Pushing his bike over dirt roads often impossible to ride on owing to the poor surface and the steepness of the gradient, he raged at race officials, shouting "Murderers!" as they awaited the much delayed race at the top of the Aubisque.

TOP: Gustave Garrigou, winner of the Tour in 1911, toils up the Col d'Aubisque.

RIGHT: Eugene Christophe's broken forks are repaired at a blacksmith's shop.

BOTTOM: Eventual winner Octave Lapize walks his bike up a mountain track in the Pyrenees during the 1910 Tour.

Boy and Bellows

In 1913 in the Pyrenees, at the bottom of the Tourmalet, an incident occurred which became one of the enduring legends of the Tour. His forks broken after being hit by a following car, Eugène Christophe shouldered his bike and walked on down to the foot of the valley and the village of Ste Marie-de-Campan, where he found a forge and set about repairing the broken forks of his machine. No help was allowed as the exhausted Christophe hammered and filed away under the strict eye of a race official. Having lost two hours, and any hope of winning the race, he finally set off to complete the stage over the Aspin and Peyresourde to the finish in Luchon. There it was announced that he had been penalised three minutes for allowing a boy to work the bellows in the forge.

INTO THE HIGH MOUNTAINS (1910–1914)

RIGHT: The notes of journalist Alphonse Steines, who was at the finish of stage 9 of the 1910 Tour, from Perpignan to Luchon.

BELOW RIGHT: The rules for the 1910 Tour, penned by Henri Desgrange, were pretty watertight and covered almost every eventuality.

By the finish it was Lapize who ran out the narrow winner over Luxembourg's François Faber, his Alcyon team-mate and the second of four Alcyon riders in the top four overall. Tragedy overshadowed the 1910 race, which suffered the Tour's first fatal incident after French rider Adolphe Hélière died, possibly from a jellyfish sting, while swimming in the sea during a rest day in Nice.

INTO THE ALPS

Longer and higher went the 1911 Tour, which at 5,344km over 15 stages (with 14 rest days) was more than twice the length of the first Tour and visited the high Alps for the first time. The field was made up of 47 independent riders and 37 team men representing four marques: La Française, Alcyon, Le Globe and Automoto. From the off the ninth edition of the Tour took a heavy toll on the favourites as 1907–08 double winner Lucien Petit-Breton crashed on the first stage from Paris to Dunkirk (351km) and both Lapize and Faber were later forced out, owing to a crash on the descent of the Ballon d'Alsace which eliminated Lapize from the race and a saddle injury which did for Faber.

The honour of crossing the mighty 2,645m-high Col du Galibier went to Emile Georget, who wheeled his machine between banks of snow on a muddy track and negotiated the long descent to win stage five from Chamonix to Grenoble (366km). Overall victory that year went to Alcyon's Gustave Garrigou, a Tour stalwart and eight-time top-ten finisher who used a single gear with a freewheel to record his one Tour victory.

Garrigou's win was not without controversy, however, as he was suspected of being involved in the poisoning of runner-up Paul Duboc of Rouen during stage 10 from Luchon to Bayonne (326km).

34

ABOVE: Henri Alavoine climbs the Col d'Allos during the 1913 Tour. The brother of four-time podium finisher Jean Alavoine was a wartime casualty, dying in 1916 at the age of 26.

BELOW: Philippe Thys on the descent of Col de Tourmalet in 1913, the year he won his first Tour.

OPPOSITE: In the mountains of the Swiss Alps during the 1913 Tour, riders chip away at the gradient, and the gaps between them, on the hairpin turns.

"The time-based classification has proven itself the only system capable of maintaining interest from start to finish."

L'AUTO, *1913*

Duboc had escaped the field but was struck down with stomach pains and vomiting which lost him the stage and valuable points in the overall. When the Tour reached Duboc's region for the penultimate stage from Cherbourg to Le Havre (361km), Garrigou rode incognito in a different jersey and with his moustache shaved off to avoid the attentions of Duboc's vengeful supporters.

THE BELGIAN ERA

Belgium recorded its first victory of the Tour in the tenth edition of 1912. Trade team numbers were capped at ten and it was accepted that team-mates could also work together and did not have to ride solo. Terrible weather followed the race, which was controlled by overall winner Odile Defraye, his Alcyon team-mates and Belgian riders keen to see a compatriot make Tour history. French opposition looked strong at the start, but Petit-Breton hit a cow on the second stage from Dunkirk to Longwy (388km) and Lapize was dropped in the Pyrenees and abandoned the race, complaining that he was outnumbered by Alcyon and the Belgians. Frenchman Eugène Christophe finished second that year and would have won the race had it been classified by time and not points.

In 1913 the Tour, for the first time since 1904, was contested on the basis of elapsed time. It failed to produce a French winner – another ten years would go by before France put a halt to Belgian victors. Riding for the all-powerful Peugeot team, which won ten of the 15 stages and produced the first three overall, the 23-year-old Belgian Philippe Thys put in a consistent performance to lead the race for the last seven stages after Nice. That year the race was run for the first time in an anti-clockwise direction, taking in the Pyrenees before the Alps.

The last Tour before the First World War took place as international events began to unfold with catastrophic speed. On the day that the Tour started, 28 June, Archduke Franz Ferdinand, heir to the Austro-Hungarian empire, was assassinated in Bosnia. Eight days after the Tour ended on 26 July, Germany declared war on France. Many Tour riders went straight into the war and never came back, including Petit-Breton, Lapize and Faber. The race itself looked a lot closer than it was, as Thys once again tenaciously held on to a 30-minute lead through the Pyrenees and Alps and looked set for a comfortable victory. On the penultimate stage from Longwy to Dunkirk (390km) a 30-minute penalty handed out to Thys after he accepted an unauthorised wheel change threw the result into doubt. The Belgian stayed glued to the wheel of France's Henri Pélissier on the final stage to Paris (340km) and emerged the narrow winner with a 1-50 lead over Pélissier.

The First World War

Continuation of the Tour de France was out of the question as the war swept across Europe and sport took a back seat to survival. Race founder Henri Desgrange threw his efforts into training army recruits before enlisting as a soldier himself, winning the Croix de Guerre. Cycles still played a part in the war, with bicycle infantries, medics, scouts and messengers. The first wearer of the yellow jersey, Eugène Christophe, served in a cycling battalion. Peace returned in November 1918, and the Tour followed seven months later, symbolising resilience and renewal as riders raced along roads scarred by battle. Sadly, many former competitors did not return. As well as three Tour champions, Emile Engel was killed ten weeks after winning a stage of the 1914 Tour and the first man to crest the Aubisque, François Lafourcade, also did not come back.

Forging into the 1920s (1919–1929)

France welcomed the Tour back with even greater enthusiasm after the First World War, but the hoped-for emergence of a great French champion was slow to materialise.

EARLY HISTORY

Only 11 riders from 67 starters finished the 13th Tour de France of 1919. It was the longest Tour to date, with 15 stages totalling 5,560km in an anti-clockwise loop that visited towns on the outermost edges of France. That the race took place at all was a credit to the drive and ingenuity of Tour founder Henri Desgrange and his organising team at *L'Auto* which pulled together large quantities of scarce racing bikes, equipment and tyres in a country ravaged by five years of war. This was also the year that the first ever yellow jersey, the *maillot jaune*, was awarded after the tenth stage from Nice to Grenoble (333km), when French

hope Eugène Christophe became the first rider to pull on the iconic symbol of race leader. Christophe was expected to win the race, having a lead of more than 28 minutes over Firmin Lambot of Belgium, but for the second time in his career his forks broke, this time on the penultimate stage from Metz to Dunkirk (468km). Once again, unaided, he repaired the fork in a forge, but he lost more than an hour, and the lead, to Lambot. The unforgiving and hated cobbled roads of the north had done to Christophe what they would do to many Tour favourites over the years, and he limped home to Paris in third place, having suffered a record number of punctures on the final day.

CHRISTOPHE CHARITY

Making the most of a French hard-luck story, *L'Auto* launched a collection for the unfortunate Christophe which raised 13,310 francs – more than he would probably have made as the winner. Belgium dominated the 1920 Tour, with 12 stage wins out of 15 and an overall winner in Philippe Thys, the first rider to win the Tour three times after his previous wins in 1913 and 1914. Belgium was confirmed as the new cycling superpower, filling the first seven places overall and controlling the race through the Pyrenees and Alps. The only non-Belgian stage winner was Henri Pélissier of France, who, like his brother Francis, was vocal in his dislike of the harshness of the Tour and of its autocratic

"Henri Pélissier has put on a show for us that is the equal of the highest artistic performance." HENRI DESGRANGE, 1923

ABOVE: Firmin Lambot remounts his bike on the Col d'Allos in the 1921 Tour.

RIGHT: Race leader Henri Pélissier shows his race face during the penultimate stage of the 1923 Tour between Metz and Dunkirk.

Henri Pélissier

Henri Pélissier was the most talented of the three Pélissier brothers, and although he won the Tour only once, in 1923, his rebellious nature and dislike of Henri Desgrange could always guarantee headlines. He was famously interviewed by French investigative journalist Albert Londres, who detailed his extensive use of stimulants and pain-killers and coined the term "les forçats de la route" (the convicts of the road) for Tour riders of the day. Pélissier rode his last Tour in 1925, but did not finish. His turbulent nature and chaotic private life dogged him to the grave. His wife, Leonie, shot herself in 1933 and, two years later, Pélissier himself was shot dead by his girlfriend, Camille, after an argument during which he slashed her with a knife.

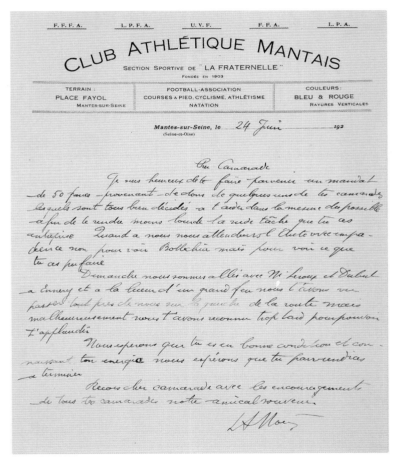

patron Desgrange. Henri Pélissier was a potential Tour winner but he had to wait another three years, while Belgians Leon Scieur, in 1921, and Lambot, in 1922, continued to crush the French opposition until 1923, 12 years after the last French victory. Henri Pélissier looked to have again lost the Tour after conceding nearly 30 minutes to the first Italian to wear the yellow jersey, Ottavio Bottecchia; but on the Alpine stages over the Cols d'Izoard, Galibier and Aravis, the Pélissier brothers out-climbed the Italian to claim the overall lead, which Henri held for the remaining five stages to Paris. Pélissier was greeted by huge crowds celebrating a French win in Paris, while sales of *L'Auto* reflected the first home win in 12 years, topping 600,000 during the race.

ITALY'S FIRST WIN

French passion for the Tour was assured, but the unpredictable Pélissier brothers could not be relied upon to deliver a second home win in 1924 when Bottecchia became the first Italian winner of the Tour after holding the yellow jersey from start to finish. Henri Pélissier and his brother had angrily abandoned the race during the third stage from Cherbourg to Brest (405km) after Henri was penalised for having discarded one of the two jerseys that he had started the stage with. Bottecchia returned in 1925 to record the double in a Tour with 18 stages, more than before but on average shorter. French influence on the race was even weaker, with one stage win and the top ten overall filled by Belgians, Luxemburgers and Italians.

The 1926 Tour de France was the longest in the history of the race. At 5,745km and with terrible weather pursuing the bunch through the Pyrenees, it was hardly surprising that only 41 of the 126 starters made it to the finish. Another Belgian, Lucien Buysse, won the first stage, from Evian (the first time the race started outside Paris) to Mulhouse (373km), then two more in the Pyrenees which cemented his lead, recorded at 1-22-25, over Luxembourg's Nicolas Frantz in Paris. Ten stages of the 1926 race had ended in bunch sprints and the race had, as was now the pattern, been decided in the Pyrenees. Because of this, as well as Desgrange's puritanical antipathy towards trade teams and informal alliances between riders, a new system of racing was

TOP: Media accreditation for Charles Faroux, writer with *L'Auto*, for 1921.

TOP LEFT: A terrible summer in the Pyrenees in 1926 made the climbs treacherous as eventual winner Lucien Buysse rode into yellow between Bayonne and Luchon.

ABOVE: Letter from members of the Mantais Cycling Club to one of their members riding in the Tour and expressing their support for him.

FORGING INTO THE 1920s (1919–1929)

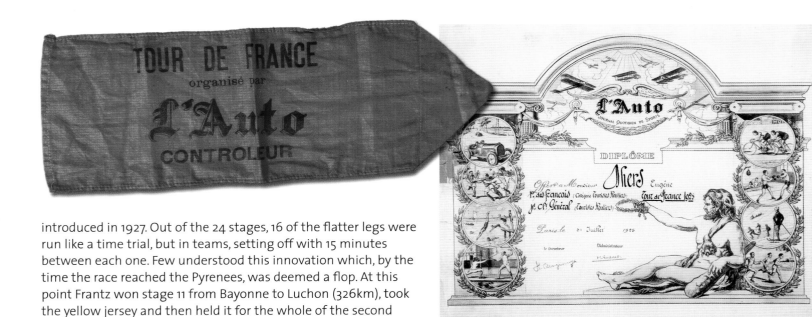

introduced in 1927. Out of the 24 stages, 16 of the flatter legs were run like a time trial, but in teams, setting off with 15 minutes between each one. Few understood this innovation which, by the time the race reached the Pyrenees, was deemed a flop. At this point Frantz won stage 11 from Bayonne to Luchon (326km), took the yellow jersey and then held it for the whole of the second half of the race.

Frantz did even better in 1928, wearing the yellow jersey as the defending champion on the first day, winning the first stage from Paris to Caen (207km) and then holding the lead for all 22 stages of the race. No other rider has ever worn yellow from before the start of stage one – as winner of the previous year's race – to the finish. Team time trial stages were still a feature of the race, but it was the mountains that again favoured the Luxemburger, who won a total of five stages that year, including the last one from Dieppe back to Paris (330km).

One of the strongest teams of the era, Alcyon, took full advantage of the 23rd Tour in 1929 when Desgrange imposed two extra team time trials to punish the bunch when the average slipped below 30kph. Alcyon won the second time trial, maintaining Belgian Maurice De Waele in the overall lead. The Flemish Tourman, second in 1927 and third in 1928, fell ill with a week to go but was supported all the way to Paris by his faithful team-mates. Afterwards Desgrange dropped the team time trials – they added little to the race and unfairly penalised strong riders on weak teams.

Ottavio Bottecchia

Ottavio Bottecchia is another winner of the Tour to suffer a violent death. Five days before the start of the 1927 Tour he was found, badly beaten, in a country lane in Italy, with his bike undamaged nearby. Various motives were explored – he was beaten for stealing grapes, was murdered by a jilted lover, or bumped off by gangsters. Bottecchia was also an anti-fascist at a time when Mussolini was head of the Italian government. A political assassination remains a plausible explanation for his demise. The Italian was married and had three children. During the First World War he was a marksman in the Italian army and escaped from prison after capture towards the end of the war. He turned professional after the war and was second overall with one stage win in his first Tour appearance in 1923.

TOP LEFT: A marshal's armband. Their power was legendary, as Eugène Christophe had found out in 1913.

TOP: A diploma awarded to Eugène Dhers in 1925, who finished 23rd overall in the Tour. He rode in ten Tours between 1912 and 1927 and completed seven of them.

ABOVE LEFT: André Leducq cuts a lonely figure during the climb up the Col du Galibier between Evian and Grenoble in 1929, the year before he won the first of his two Tours.

LEFT: Ottavio Bottecchia during the 1923 Tour de France.

OPPOSITE: Jef Demuysere, André Leduoq and Charles Pélissier all left their mark on the Tour throughout the 1920s and 1930s.

The 1930s Revolution (1929–1939)

This was the decade when the Tour left the old era behind and evolved into an event with classifications and tactics that have shaped Tours to this day.

A key moment in the Tour's history came in 1930: this was when Tour founder Henri Desgrange introduced teams to the race – a change that would profoundly affect all grand tours henceforth. Desgrange was motivated by the lack of French success in the race – there had been no French winner since Henri Pélissier in 1923 – and by his dislike of squads of riders backed by bicycle companies that had ensured a string of winners from Belgium, Italy and Luxembourg. Sales of his sports newspaper, *L'Auto*, which had been the organiser and official record of the Tour from its inception, were also slipping.

At a stroke Desgrange banished the trade teams and offered places in his race exclusively to national and regional squads. In 1930 the Tour was contested by teams from France, Belgium, Italy, Spain and Germany, plus regional teams made up of individual entrants called *touristes-routiers*. In the absence of bikes supplied by the former backers of the trade teams, Desgrange supplied the field with identical machines painted yellow, and ditched the rule that forbade riders on the same team to help each other

after a puncture or equipment failure. To cover the increased costs of kitting out and supporting unsponsored national and regional teams, Desgrange sold road space in front of the race to a travelling convoy of advertisers, known as the *caravane publicitaire*. The introduction of eight-man teams, collaboration between team-mates and the publicity caravan are elements of the race that remain more or less intact today. Other innovations made throughout the 1930s also survive, such as shorter stages, numbering 20 or more, which started and finished during the working day; time bonuses for stage winners; and a points system, *le grand prix de la montagne*, to find the best climber.

"The fatigue is nothing, the pain isn't much more, but the fear of not winning was truly horrible to me."

ANTONIN MAGNE, 1931

OPPOSITE: Tour winner Georges Speicher and Learco Guerra, second overall, ride together on the Tarbes to Pau stage 18 of the 1933 Tour.

LEFT: VIP Tour de France pass with leather strap.

BELOW: Antonin Magne, who did not ride in the 1932 Tour, assists his friend André Leducq in the climb up the Aubisque.

Antonin Magne

Antonin Magne won the Tour in 1931 and 1934, his two wins due in part to training rides in the Pyrenees and selfless teamwork by his French national team. In the 1934 race Magne held on to the yellow jersey in the Pyrenees thanks to his team-mate, a former hotel bell-boy René Vietto. First Vietto gave up his wheel, and then on stage 16 from Ax-les-Thermes to Luchon (165km) he turned around on the road to follow the race route back to Magne, who needed Vietto's bike after his own was broken. Magne went on to win the Tour but it was the story of Vietto, who finished fifth overall and might have challenged Magne had it not been for team orders, on which *L'Auto* lavished its most florid praise.

REFINED TACTICS

Racing tactics became ever more sophisticated, with team riders or *domestiques* protecting and shepherding their designated team leaders. The bunch was now used as a sanctuary, and as a base from which to launch strategic attacks. Gone were the days of individuals setting off on lonely 400km treks through the night.

Advances in equipment also enabled the field to stay together and to climb and descend the high mountains. In 1937 derailleur gears were allowed for the first time, and many riders took advantage of the multiple gear shift system that enabled riders to make gear changes on the move – a marked advance on the old method of dismounting and flipping the rear wheel to use the second of two sprockets. Brakes on the front and rear wheels also made descending a more precise and acrobatic, though not necessarily safer activity.

In the 1935 Tour the Spanish rider Francisco Cepeda became the first rider to die while racing in the Tour, sustaining fatal injuries after crashing on the descent of the Galibier. Since then two more riders have died during stages of the Tour, also in the mountains: Tom Simpson on the ascent of Mont Ventoux in 1967 and Fabio Casartelli on the descent of the Col de Portet d'Aspet in 1995.

FRANCE'S FABULOUS FIVE

Desgrange's changes had a lasting effect on continental cycle racing, and for the first five years of the 1930s also produced French winners, which ensured the long-term popularity of the Tour in France. The circulation of *L'Auto* revived spectacularly and in 1933 hit a record 854,000. From 1936 paid holidays introduced by the Popular Front government guaranteed a festive roadside audience in every corner of France. For four years they had French winners to cheer on: André Leducq in 1930 and 1932, Antonin Magne in 1931 and 1934 and Georges Speicher in 1933. Well-drilled French teams with brilliant individual riders such as René Vietto, who sacrificed a high overall placing after giving up his bike to Magne in 1934, were key to the French successes. Once again, it was Belgium that broke the French victory run, with Romain

Maes and the unrelated Sylvère Maes winning in 1935 and 1936 before Roger Lapébie restored order by winning for France in 1937, using a derailleur gear on every stage.

Having abandoned the race after falling into an icy stream in 1937, Italian ace Gino Bartali smashed the field in the 1938 race. He attacked on stage 14 from Digne to Briançon (218km), with a solo ride through the Alps which put 17 minutes into his closest rival, Félicien Vervaecke of Belgium. Bartali became only the second Italian to win the Tour after Ottavio Bottecchia's double in 1924–25, but as the Second World War loomed in 1939 the absence of teams from Italy and Germany, as well as injury to French favourite Lapébie, allowed Belgian Sylvère Maes to score his second Tour win over the heroic Vietto, who battled to second with bronchitis but had no answer to Maes's climbing in the Alps. That year marked the end of the inter-war era, and thirty years were to pass before Belgium produced another Tour winner.

TOP LEFT: There were official and unofficial songs for and about the Tour de France. This is sheet music for a new song penned to celebrate André Leducq's victory in 1932.

TOP RIGHT: Belgian Romain Maes interrupted the French party when he won the Tour in 1935, wearing the yellow jersey from the end of the first day all the way to Paris.

ABOVE: Tour de France souvenir plates depicting scenes from Tours in the 1930s.

Sylvère Maes

Sylvère Maes, "the sly guy", won the last Tour de France before the outbreak of the Second World War. The 1939 Tour was boycotted by Germany and Italy, and Spain did not attend after the civil war, but Maes, who won the Tour in 1936, overcame an ailing René Vietto in the Pyrenees and took the yellow jersey after impressive riding over the Col d'Izoard and winning the first ever Tour mountain time trial up the Col d'Iseran. Maes's winning time set a new record average speed of 31.9kph, just under 20mph. Maes was the owner of a café in his native Flanders which he named "Tourmalet", after the great Pyrenean climb.

ABOVE: Gino Bartali forges a lonely path in the Col d'Izoard on his way to winning the 1938 Tour.

LEFT: Belgian racing cyclist Sylvere Maes celebrating his Tour de France victory in 1939.

Wartime Hiatus (1940–1947)

The Second World War brought a temporary halt to the Tour de France and a string of shortened replacement races, but hunger for the real thing remained.

As the Germany army thundered into France and war swept across Europe again, the 1940 edition of the Tour de France was cast into doubt.

The UCI, the sport's international governing body, had issued dates for the race, which clashed with the Tour of Germany. Dismayed, Desgrange refused to put on the race and died a year later. In June 1940, eleven months after Sylvère Maes had entered Paris as winner, German forces were marching past the Arc de Triomphe. The Tour de France was not held between 1940 and 1946, the longest hiatus in the race's history.

In the years that followed, the German occupiers put pressure on race director and *L'Auto* journalist Jacques Goddet to hold the race in order to boost morale – and win propaganda points – but he refused. The Tour should be an honourable, happy event, not take place under a cloud. A protégé of Desgrange, who saw him as a son, Goddet became Tour director in 1936 as illness affected the race's founder. In later years, Goddet was a recognisable figure on the race for his khaki shorts and pith helmet. In 1942 and 1943, he whetted the appetite of *L'Auto* readers for the real deal by asking them to vote for a fantasy French team to ride an imagined Tour de France.

SLIMMED-DOWN SUBSTITUTES

Invasion caused a halt to most big races in France. The country was split in half, the southern part administered by the collaborating government, Vichy France, and the northern part occupied by German troops. Rationing and privation made for subdued, shortened races serving as substitutes for the Tour.

The Circuit de France, held in September 1942, was one such competition, held by collaborationist newspaper *La France Socialiste*.

Belgian François Neuville won, but the event was poorly organised, with shabby accommodation and miscalculated scheduling. One stage had an official waving a handkerchief in near darkness outside Clermont-Ferrand to signify the stage's impromptu finish there, rather than within the city.

In 1943 *L'Auto* organised a Grand Prix du Tour de France, a season-long competition comprising nine one-day races, including the famous one-day Classics Paris–Roubaix and Paris–Tours. Jo Goutorbe won the event that year, and Maurice de Simpelaere was leading the 1944 competition when it was interrupted by a happy event: France's liberation.

Fewer of the Tour's cyclists saw frontline action in the Second World War compared to the First, because of the shift away from trench warfare and the rapid advance of the German army.

But the stars of the Tour still had to face up to the realities of war. Two days after winning the Tour of Italy in 1940, future two-time Tour champion Fausto Coppi was called up to serve in the Italian army. He was allowed to train and race three days a week as long as he made it back to the barracks by curfew. Coppi fought on the African front and was captured by the Allies in April 1943. Serving as a mechanic, lorry cleaner and batman, he was well treated, though he returned home in 1945 to discover that all his pre-war savings had been converted into Italian government bonds and were worthless.

Coppi's great Italian rival and 1938 Tour champion Gino Bartali helped Jewish refugees. He hid documents used to make false identity papers in his bicycle frame and saddle, and he would ride around Tuscany, getting through checkpoints on the pretence of being on a 380km training ride.

Andrea Carrea

Andrea Carrea was a hard-working team-mate of Fausto Coppi. Just getting to the Tour de France start line was a triumph over adversity for him. He was interned in Buchenwald, the German concentration camp, during the Second World War and survived two death marches. Returning home emaciated and malnourished, Carrea was working as a mason when Coppi's brother Serse recommended him to take up cycling in 1945. A consummate *domestique*, his loyalties to his team and to his leader Coppi were so strong that when he won the yellow jersey during the 1952 Tour de France while marshalling a breakaway, he burst into tears and apologised to Coppi. The next day he relinquished it to his leader, who won on L'Alpe d'Huez when the race visited the mountain for the first time.

LEFT: Gino Bartali alongside Andrea Carrea at the Tour de France in 1952.

OPPOSITE: Jean Robic, the pugnacious Frenchman, was the first post-war Tour winner in 1947.

A RETURN TO NORMALITY

After liberation, France changed governments as if they were light-bulbs, having nine between 1945 and the beginning of 1949. The Tour organisation underwent its own shake-up too. *L'Auto*, seen as collaborationist, was closed by the government and a replacement sprang up: *L'Equipe*, the daily sports newspaper which has become synonymous with the Tour.

Rights for the Tour de France went to the government, and *L'Equipe* faced competition to host the Tour from the magazine amalgam of *Sports* and *Miroir-Sprint*. Both held competing five-stage races in 1946. The Course du Tour de France, put on by *L'Equipe* and *Le Parisien Libéré*, ran from Monaco to Paris and was won by callow climber Apo Lazarides, ahead of his leader René Vietto. It was better received than their rival's Ronde de France and included the national team format that had captured the public's pre-war imagination. They went on to organise the 1947 race after the rights had been given to the Parc des Princes in an attempt at compromise.

The Tour was back. That it even started again in a country beset by rampant shortages, heavy rationing, towns levelled by bombing and a weakened transportation infrastructure, was victory in itself. It underlined the beginning of a return to normality and resumed its role as a symbol of France's own reconstruction, of freedom and celebration.

"The Tour heralds the return of joie de vivre. It spontaneously establishes an entirely free community, it brings people together in a good-natured way that makes no distinctions of class or political affiliation."

JACQUES GODDET

LEFT: A letter from Karel Van Wynendaele, regarding a rival Tour started while the Tour de France was suspended during World War 2.

BELOW: A bill from P. Chaplais, wholesale grocer, for provisions on the 1947 Tour, the first after World War 2.

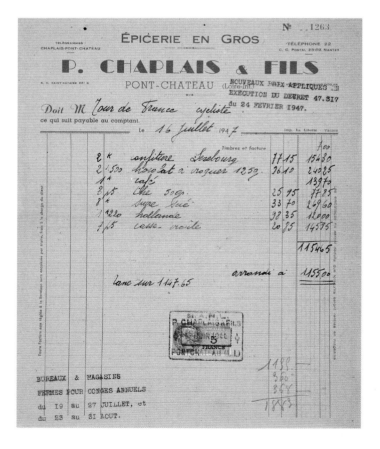

OPPOSITE: The legendary Italian rider Fausto Coppi leads his compatriot and rival Gino Bartali in the Pyrenees on a stage between Pau and Luchon. Both Coppi and Bartali won the Tour twice each, Coppi in 1949 and 1952, Bartali in 1938 and 1948, during an era when Italians ruled the race.

The Golden Era

Some of the greatest and most charismatic stars of cycling emerged in the immediate post-war years, when the Tour drew huge crowds hungry for the innocent pleasures of sporting competition. It certainly helped that France was producing Tour winners like Louison Bobet, Jacques Anquetil and Bernard Hinault. Super-champions all, now add Fausto Coppi and Eddy Merckx – what an era!

LEFT: Jacques Anquetil (centre) rides the Col du Tourmalet during the 1957 edition, cheered on by a massive, partisan crowd. The Norman crushed the opposition to win his first Tour de France, winning four individual stages as well as the team time trial.

Italian Dominance (1948–1952)

Post-war Tours drew enormous crowds as great sporting rivalries thrilled the fans once again. The Tour also continued to evolve, with the addition of new routes through mountain passes and the introduction of television coverage.

There was no Tour de France in 1946, just a year after the end of the Second World War, and the 1947 "Tour of the Liberation" was won by the short, combative Breton Jean Robic from a peloton of riders most of whom had no experience of the Tour. Twelve months later a more competitive field assembled for the 35th edition, which introduced changes that marked a return to confidence in "La Grande Boucle" (The Big Loop). There were four new stage towns and the race also made excursions into Switzerland, Italy and Belgium. Among the mountain passes included for the first time were the Turini, Forclaz and Vue des Alpes. The most portentous change was the presence of television cameras at the finish in Paris, opening up the Tour to a wider audience for the first time in its history.

Gino "The Pious" Bartali won the 1948 Tour, at the age of 34, ten years after his first victory in 1938. Before the war the Italian, a devout Catholic, had a reputation as a pure climber, but he returned with a strong sprint in his arsenal to win six stages, distancing second-placed Alberic Schotte of Belgium by 26-16. Bartali had been more than 20 minutes down after stage 12 and

the story of his fightback has passed into Tour folklore.

Back in his native Italy the attempted assassination of the chairman of the Communist Party had precipitated a general strike and fears of civil war. The night before the 274km stage 13 from Cannes to Briançon, Bartali was telephoned by the leader of the Christian Democrat Party who urged him to divert attention in Italy by winning a stage of the Tour. Next day an inspired Bartali took off alone and crossed the Col d'Izoard with more than 18 minutes' advantage on the yellow jersey, the 23-year-old French prodigy Louison Bobet.

BARTALI DELAYS DISORDER
At the line Bartali gave Italy a stage win that put Italian disorder on hold and moved the Tour veteran to within 51 seconds of Bobet's yellow jersey. That guaranteed another day of peace across the border as the whole of Italy sat glued to their wirelesses while Bartali and Bobet went head to head over a 263km stage across the Lautaret, Galibier and Croix de Fer. Bobet could hold Bartali no longer as they left Grenoble, and Bartali

"His long legs extend to the pedals with the joints of a gazelle. At the end of each pedal stroke his ankles flex gracefully – all the moving parts turn in oil."

ANDRÉ LEDUCQ, CONTEMPORARY OF COPPI

BELOW LEFT: The stands of the Parc des Princes in Paris are packed as the 1949 Tour de France reaches its climax.

BELOW: Ferdi Kübler powers to victory in the final time trial of the 1950 Tour which he won by more than nine minutes from Stan Ockers.

Fausto Coppi

Of all the great champions Fausto Coppi remains one of the most revered and legendary. The record of "Il Campionissimo" was interrupted by the Second World War and his two Tour de France wins are well short of the five of Anquetil, Merckx, Hinault and Indurain. It was the manner of his wins combined with his physical frailties that continue to fascinate. In 1949 Coppi became the first rider to win the Tour of Italy and the Tour de France in the same year, and he repeated the feat in 1952. His Tour record included nine stage wins and 19 days in the yellow jersey. Coppi's affair with a married woman scandalised 1950s Italy and sharply divided supporters of the atheist Coppi from fans of the devout Bartali. In 1960, after contracting malaria on a hunting trip to Africa, Coppi died aged 40.

ABOVE: After Gino Bartali won in 1948, Coppi walked away with the Tour in 1949 and 1952. This is a contemporary caricature of *Il Campionissimo*.

ABOVE LEFT: The *Directeur Sportif's* licence for Antonin Magne, winner of Le Tour in 1931 and 1934 and a team manager after World War 2.

BELOW: Gino Bartali leads Fausto Coppi in the Alps during the 1949 Tour, which Coppi went on to win at his first attempt.

rode alone over the Col de Porte and into Aix-les-Bains with an overall advantage over Bobet of 8-03. An Italian was in yellow, the general strike was called off and Bartali won a further two stages as he consolidated his lead on the road back to Paris.

Bobet was not the only rising star waiting to burst on to the Tour scene. In 1949 Fausto Coppi, a willowy, pigeon-chested Italian who had already won the Tour of Italy twice, made his Tour debut on the same team as Bartali. At 29 Coppi was at the height of his powers, which few could match against the clock or in the mountains. With Coppi and Bartali partnered on the Italian team the potential for schism was all too real, and it took all the diplomatic skills of *directeur sportif* and former Tourman Alfredo Binda to broker a fragile entente between them. When Coppi crashed in Brittany on stage five, losing 36 minutes, Binda once again stepped in, this time to persuade the forlorn Coppi to stay in the race. In the Alps Bartali and Coppi left the field in tatters over the mountains to Briançon, where Bartali took the yellow jersey. But stage 17 the next day from Briançon to St Vincent d'Aosta in Italy saw the old order toppled as a puncture to Bartali on the Petit-Saint-Bernard climb gave Coppi free rein to forge ahead, deposing Bartali from the lead. He made certain of victory in the 137km final time trial from Colmar to Nancy, increasing his final lead over second-placed Bartali to 10-55.

With Coppi injured and a non-starter, the 1950 Tour favoured Bartali as he and a powerful Italian team entered the Pyrenees. On stage 11 from Pau to St Gaudens, however, angry French crowds

ITALIAN DOMINANCE (1948–1952)

threw stones at Bartali, who crashed when the road was blocked by a mob near to the finish. That night, despite Fiorenzo Magni being in yellow and Bartali's sixth place overall, the Italian team withdrew from the race. Switzerland's Ferdi Kübler inherited the lead and held off spirited long-range attacks from Bobet all the way to Paris.

Hugo Koblet thrilled Swiss fans when he succeeded Kübler in 1951 to become the second Swiss winner in Tour history. A masterful solo victory on stage 11 from Brive-la-Gaillarde to Agen put time into Coppi, Bobet and Bartali and moved him up to third overall. On stage 14 Koblet won a two-man sprint into Luchon ahead of Coppi, whose fluctuating form was attributed to grief at the death of his brother Serse in a racing accident. Koblet held the yellow jersey from there to the finish, his assured and stylish riding earning him the nickname "The Pedaller of Charm".

COPPI'S MASTERCLASS

Two shorter time trials and the addition for the first time of the now legendary L'Alpe d'Huez, as well as first ascents of Sestriere and the Puy de Dôme, gave the 1952 race a flavour of Tours of the modern era. Traditional marathon stages, however, ensured that the peloton would pedal 1,500km further than today's professionals, which suited Coppi just fine as he set about the most crushing of his two Tour wins.

With his great rivals all missing from the Tour through illness, and with Bartali no longer a contender and happy even to give Coppi his wheel after he punctured three times on stage 11, Coppi waited until the Alpe d'Huez stage 10 to win the stage and claim yellow. The next day he won at Sestriere, increasing his overall lead to nearly 20 minutes. At this point the organisers doubled the prize money for second place to encourage the demoralised peloton, such was the dominance of "Il Campionissimo" (Champion of Champions). Coppi won stages to Pau and on the Puy de Dôme to run out the winner in Paris 28-17 ahead of Constant "Stan" Ockers of Belgium, a post-war record winning margin that still stands today.

BELOW: Fausto Coppi wins the first ever stage to L'Alpe d'Huez in 1952.

BOTTOM: Gino Bartali wins the 1948 Tour de France.

OPPOSITE: Italy's two great rivals, Gino Bartali (left) and Fausto Coppi, observe a temporary truce by sharing what looks like a bottle of wine.

Gino Bartali

Gino Bartali won the Tour de France in 1938 and two Tours of Italy before the Second World War. He won a third Tour of Italy in 1946, and made history in 1948 by winning his second Tour de France, ten years after the first. Small, powerful, and with the face of a boxer, Bartali was a brilliant climber whose tough reputation earned him the nickname "The Iron Man". He also was a devout Catholic and famously attended Mass every day of the Tour. His rivalry with compatriot Fausto Coppi filled pages in the Italian sports press and although there were big differences between them off the bike, on the road they were good team-mates. He even gave a wheel to Coppi after he punctured during the 1952 Tour, helping Coppi towards his second Tour win.

The Bobet Era (1953–1956)

The 50th year of the Tour de France marked the start of the first of three consecutive Tour wins by the brave but prickly Breton Louison Bobet.

Louison Bobet came to the 1953 Tour as an experienced and strong favourite, having ridden in five Tours previously and crossed swords many times with Fausto Coppi, Ferdi Kübler and Hugo Koblet. Coppi, having won the Tour of Italy a month before, had decided not to ride in France, and although Bobet had also ridden and retired on the final stage with saddle soreness (which plagued his career), he joined a strong but quarrelsome French national squad for the start in Strasbourg.

One of the stars riding for a French regional team was the 1947 Tour winner, Jean Robic. He took advantage of the opportunity and after winning stage 11 to Luchon, the accident-prone Frenchman, who wore a curious helmet made from strips of rubber, found himself in yellow. Stung into action by Robic's ambush, the French national team went on to the attack on stage 13, causing the yellow jersey to lose nearly 40 minutes as Bobet moved to third overall. Bobet then staked his claim as leader of the French team with an epic ride over the Col d'Izoard on stage 18 from Gap to Briançon. He arrived at the line with five minutes' advantage over the rest, which he then held until the finish to record a long-awaited first Tour win. Also feted in Paris was the first winner of the green jersey for points, Fritz Schaer of Switzerland.

To celebrate the 50th anniversary of the Tour the organisers invited 15 former winners including the 82-year-old Maurice Garin, winner of the inaugural 1903 Tour. Another former Tour winner rolled into Paris for the last time: Gino Bartali's 11th place was a worthy performance from the 39-year-old Italian champion.

In 1954 Amsterdam became the first town outside France to host Le Départ in the history of the Tour. With Coppi injured and the Italian team absent after a squabble over sponsorship, the

ABOVE: Bobet is urged on by French team manager Marcel Bidot during stage 11, from Marseilles to Avignon, of the 1955 Tour.

TOP: Bobet and Charly Gaul (right) go head to head in 1955 on the stage from St Gaudens to Pau.

Louison Bobet

Louison Bobet was the first rider to win a hat-trick of Tours. Philippe Thys was the only other rider to have won three – in 1913, 1914 and 1920 – but they were not consecutive. Born in 1925 to the son of a Breton baker, Bobet worked long hours in the family business and was possessed of a work ethic and a will to succeed that ensured a dazzling career on the bike. Apart from his Tour victories he was also a superb rider of the one-day classics and was the first French winner of the Tour of Flanders in 1955. He wore the rainbow jersey of World Road Race Champion after puncturing and chasing back to win at the Solingen circuit in Germany in 1954 and took a prized victory in the Paris–Roubaix race of 1956.

FACTFILE

Born	12 March 1925 Saint-Meen le Grand, France
Died	13 March 1983, Biarritz, France France
Team Tour Wins	1953 – 2 stage wins
	1954 – 3 stage wins
	1955 – 2 stage wins
Other Tours	1947 – dnf
	1948 – 4th – 2 stage wins
	1949 – dnf
	1950 – 3rd – KoM – 1 stage
	1951 – 20th – 1 stage win
	1958 – 7th
	1959 – dnf

54

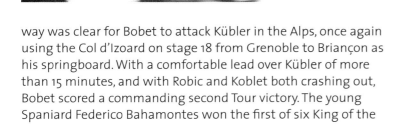

55

way was clear for Bobet to attack Kübler in the Alps, once again using the Col d'Izoard on stage 18 from Grenoble to Briançon as his springboard. With a comfortable lead over Kübler of more than 15 minutes, and with Robic and Koblet both crashing out, Bobet scored a commanding second Tour victory. The young Spaniard Federico Bahamontes won the first of six King of the

ABOVE: Bobet's wife, Christiane, cheers on her husband in the final time trial of the 1953 Tour.

BELOW: Jean Mallejac is treated by Tour doctor Pierre Dumas after collapsing on Mont Ventoux in 1955.

RIGHT: Entitled "Au Petit Tour … niquet", this preview of the 1956 Tour suggested that finding a winner would be like picking Lotto numbers (it was Roger Walkowiak).

illust. par BERNARD BUFFET

PARIS
ARRIVÉE

24ᵉ Etape - 19 Juillet 1958

PAU
18ᵉ Étape - 26 Juillet 1955

Illustration VAN DONGEN

56

LEFT: Kees Van Dongen produced a postcard for the 18th stage of the 1955 Tour, from Saint-Gaudens to Pau.

FAR LEFT: Jacques Anquetil, portrayed by Bernard Buffet in 1958, but Charly Gaul wore yellow in Paris that year.

BELOW: Jean Robic crashed out of the 1954 Tour on the road to Caen. His helper carries Robic's distinctive leather crash hat.

Mountains titles, making a name for himself right from the start when he pointedly stopped at the top of one of the climbs and ate an ice-cream while he waited for the rest of the peloton labouring on the slopes below.

THE TOUR ON TV

In 1955 recorded TV images of the 43rd Tour de France were transmitted for the first time to French homes. A transfer between Poitiers and Châtellerault for the penultimate stage also marked the first break in the continuous chain of stages that had characterised previous Tours. The route in total was 4,479km long, some 400km less than previous editions but still about 1,000km longer than modern Tours.

Bobet was once again the outstanding favourite, but there were doubts over his participation due to the worsening injury to his saddle area. He did not help himself much either, having an irascible and driven nature which irked team-mates and divided French bike fans. Persuaded to ride by French team manager Marcel Bidot, Bobet once again waited until one of the "queen stages", this time over Mont Ventoux in Provence, to put in a virtuoso performance and stake a claim to his third Tour. Bobet came off a baking hot Ventoux to win stage 11 into Avignon, while behind him both Kübler and Jean Mallejac succumbed to the heat and probably dope-induced over-exertion – a portent of the tragic death of Tom Simpson in the same place 12 years later.

"Out of all three, this one was the one with the most prizes; the prizes of courage and will."

LOUISON BOBET, 1955 TOUR WINNER

While Bobet rode heroically into yellow on stage 17 from Toulouse to St Gaudens, the stage was won by a slightly-built climber from Luxembourg who excelled in bad weather. Charly Gaul won stages in the Alps and Pyrenees and threatened to make an overall challenge until the Ventoux stage, where the hot sun melted his climbing wings. Bobet's nearest rival was Jean Brankart, from Belgium, who won the final time trial and closed to four minutes 53 seconds before the final stage the following day on to the Parc des Princes track in Paris.

WALKOWIAK'S SURPRISE WIN

Bobet's saddle injury, which required 150 stitches in an operation at the end of the year, prevented him from starting the 1956 Tour, and with Robic injured again, and Coppi, Kübler and Koblet non-starters, the race had a transitional feel to it. It suited an unfancied rider like Roger Walkowiak, riding for the French North East Central (NEC) team, who made the most of an 18-minute advantage gained after a 31-rider breakaway group escaped on stage seven. French national team riders André Darrigade and Gilbert Bauvin fell out over how to tackle Walkowiak, while the modest all-rounder continued to climb with Bahamontes through the Alps to Grenoble, where he took the yellow jersey after stage 18, won by Gaul. Walkowiak won no stages in the Tour, but he had done enough to lead Bauvin by 1-25 when the race arrived in Paris four days later, having achieved a record average speed of 36.268kmh.

LEFT: At the Parc des Princes track in Paris Bobet celebrates his first Tour win in 1953.

BELOW: 1951 Tour de France winner Hugo Koblet, pictured here in 1954.

Hugo Koblet

Just when everyone thought that Fausto Coppi was the coolest bike rider in the peloton, along came a Swiss ace who was elegance personified. Hugo Koblet was the first foreign winner of the Giro d'Italia in 1950 and his victory in the 1951 Tour de France was as complete a display of all-round class as has ever been seen. Koblet, famous for his matinee idol looks and the comb that he carried in his jersey pocket to restore them at stage finishes, was a smooth and fluid rider who was not afraid to strike out on lone solo escapes. Not for nothing was he nicknamed "The Pedaller of Charm". Koblet retired in 1958 and died in a car crash in 1964, aged 39. Suicide was suspected as witnesses saw his white Alfa Romeo being driven at speed into a tree on the road to Esslingen.

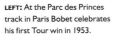

The Anquetil Era (1957–1968)

This was the era of the great climbers, a super but fractious French team, and a brilliant champion from Normandy destined to be the first rider to win the Tour five times.

The Tour debut of the 23-year-old Jacques Anquetil in 1957 was eagerly awaited and, such was the morale and strength of the French national team, expectations of a maiden victory were high. Anquetil's astonishing ability to ride solo had already established him as an unbeatable time triallist and, despite two years out of the sport while he did military service in Algeria in 1954–55, the Norman came to the 1957 Tour as an outstanding favourite. Three-times winner Louison Bobet was not on the French team – after winning the Tour of Italy he could not face another gruelling Tour, meanwhile signalling by his absence that Anquetil was the new face of French cycling. Anquetil did not disappoint. He won stage four into his home city of Rouen and pulled on his first yellow jersey two days later in Charleroi. He lost the jersey a day later but, after joining a long breakaway on stage nine from Besançon to Thonon les Bains, he won the stage and the next day over the Galibier to Briançon took the overall lead from his team-mate Jean Forestier. Overcoming a bout of "hunger knock" in the Pyrenees, Anquetil would remain in yellow to Paris, winning the two time trials to finish nearly 15 minutes ahead of second-placed Marcel Janssens of Belgium.

"I renounced everything, even the Classics, to win the Tour de France."

JACQUES ANQUETIL

The following two years of the Tour were dominated by two of the greatest climbers that cycling has ever seen. Anquetil was ill during the 1958 Tour and his intense rivalry with fellow countryman Roger Rivière partly explains how Charly Gaul and Federico Bahamontes managed to overcome "Maître Jacques" in consecutive years. But that should not detract from Gaul's peerless climbing in terrible weather on stage 21 from Briançon to Aix-les-Bains and his fine time trial two days later that sealed the Luxemburger's one and only Tour win in 1958. The following year Bahamontes certainly profited from the Anquetil–Rivière stalemate, which allowed the Spaniard to recover from a four-

BOTTOM LEFT: Experienced Gastone Nencini won the 1960 Tour after his main rival Roger Rivière crashed out sustaining a career-ending broken back.

BELOW: Charly Gaul and Jacques Anquetil ride side-by-side during the 1961 Tour.

LEFT: Novelty Raymond Poulidor ballpoint pen. The cap has his sponsor's name on it: Mercier.

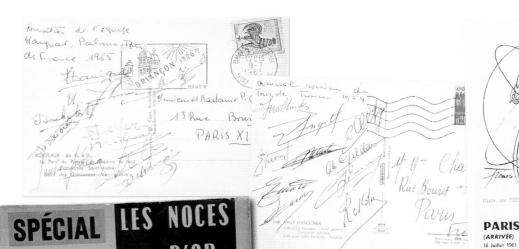

SPÉCIAL **LES NOCES D'OR DU TOUR**

GRATUIT

L. BOBET BP Hutchinson

HELVET LEROUX

ANQUETIL BATTRA-T-IL LE RECORD DE BOBET ?

édité par Sport Vie

1F 50 SUPPLÉMENT AU N° 83 JUIN 1963

PARIS
(ARRIVÉE)
16 Juillet 1961

TOUR DE FRANCE CYCLISTE 1961

Illustr. par TRÉMOIS

RIS
(ARRIVÉE)
17
7
60

FRANCE CYCLISTE 1960

Grav. Landier

ABOVE: A collection of postcards (left) signed by a group of riders after they had completed a stage in Bordeaux 1964. (above) signed by a group of riders after they had completed a stage in Andorra 1964. (top right) Tsuguharu Foujita celebrated the Arivée Finale in Paris in 1960. (top middle) Jacques Anquetil, depicted arriving in Paris in 1961, by Pierre-Yves Trémois.

LEFT: "Can Anquetil (right) better the record of Bobet?" asks this Tour special magazine.

BELOW LEFT: Jacques Anquetil is seen here heading for his second TT stage win on the road to Périgueux, near the end of the 1961 Tour.

minute deficit on stage 18. "The Eagle of Toledo" jumped on the chance to capitalise on the feuding Frenchmen and won the stage 15 mountain time trial to the Puy de Dôme before climbing decisively into the yellow jersey through the Alps.

TRIUMPH AND TRAGEDY

Italian Gastone Nencini won the 1960 Tour, a race marred by a crash that paralysed Roger Rivière. The French track star had filled Anquetil's place as team leader after Anquetil had elected not to start, having won the Tour of Italy just 17 days before. Nencini and Rivière duelled for the lead on stage 14 from Millau to Avignon with the wily Italian setting an infernal pace on the descents. Rivière, an indifferent bike handler, left the road on the descent of the Perjuret, sustaining a broken back which ended his career.

Jacques Anquetil

Jacques Anquetil may have been France's first superstar of the Tour, but his aloof manner and calculating style resulted in a cool relationship with the French public. Born the son of a strawberry and apple farmer in Quincampoix near Rouen, Anquetil cultivated the image of a bon viveur by allowing stories to circulate about his love of good food and wine. He would be seen at barbecues on rest days and was known to eat plates of shellfish washed down with a bottle of Muscadet during the Tour. Whether these were ruses to psych out his rivals or the behaviour of a maverick is open to doubt – most likely a bit of both. Outspoken and unrepentant on the subject of doping, Anquetil was against testing, claiming that it was not possible to race for 200 days a year without drugs. He died of cancer aged 53.

FACTFILE

Born	8 January 1934, Mont Saint Aignan, France
Died	18 November 1987, Rouen, France
Team	French National
Tour Wins	1957 – 4 stage wins, 1961 – 2 stage wins, 1962 – 2 stage wins, 1963 – 4 stage wins, 1964 – 4 stage wins
Other Tours	1958 – dnf, 1959 – 3rd, 1966 – dnf

THE ANQUETIL ERA (1957–1968)

ANQUETIL'S ASCENDANCY

In 1961 Anquetil returned to the Tour determined to take up where he left off in 1957. Two stages were held on the first day of the Tour, the second a 28.5km time trial around Versailles which Anquetil duly won and which earned him the yellow jersey. From there until Paris, twenty stages later, the Norman

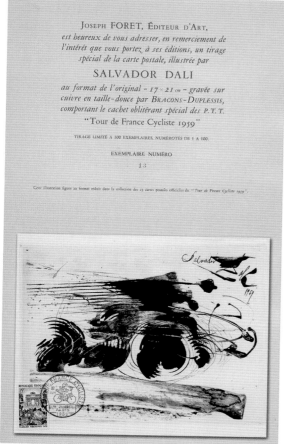

LEFT: Spanish aritist Salvador Dalí, in his inimitable style, drew a postcard for the 1959 Tour which came with a protective wrapper.

BELOW: The ever-popular Raymond Poulidor is featured on this key ring.

BOTTOM RIGHT: Tom Simpson is close to collapse on the Ventoux during the 1967 Tour.

OPPOSITE: Anquetil and Poulidor play out their fierce duel on the Puy de Dôme in 1964.

maintained his overall lead, joining Ottavio Bottecchia, Nicolas Frantz and Romain Maes as the only riders to wear yellow from day one to the finish. A year later Anquetil scored his third Tour win with a patient ride which kept his rivals on a short leash until the final time trial on stage 20 from Bourgoin to Lyons, where he cut loose and, catching Raymond Poulidor for three minutes, vaulted into the lead with two days to go. In 1962 Tom Simpson became the first Briton to wear the yellow jersey, ending the Tour in sixth overall place.

Anquetil's fourth and fifth Tour wins confirmed him as a great climber as well as time triallist. Shorter time trials had been introduced to give less of an advantage to the Norman, but in both Tours he rode the high mountains alongside his main rivals Bahamontes and Poulidor. In 1964 he went head to head with Poulidor on a legendary stage 20 from Brive to the Puy de Dôme. Riding elbow to elbow in the cycling equivalent of a contact sport Anquetil assured victory by matching Poulidor until close to the line. Victory in the final stage time trial saw him run out the victor just 55 seconds ahead of "Poupou".

The Tours from 1965 to 1968 marked an interregnum. Anquetil skipped the 1965 Tour, won by the 22-year-old Italian phenomenon Felice Gimondi, and supported Lucien Aimar in his final Tour in 1966 when he retired from the race suffering from bronchitis. A year later another talented Frenchman, Roger Pingeon, maintained the French claim to their national event. That was the year Simpson died on Mont Ventoux, confirming what many had feared was an inevitable consequence of doping in the peloton. Jan Janssen became the first Dutchman to win the Tour in 1968, dubbed by the organisers "Le Tour de la Santé" (The Tour of Health). Gimondi stayed away and the brightest new star in the firmament, a young Belgian called Eddy Merckx, also missed the Tour, having won the Tour of Italy earlier in June.

61

Raymond Poulidor

Raymond Poulidor was an exceptional cyclist whose inability to win the Tour de France hung over him like a cloud throughout a distinguished 17-year career. He finished second three times and third five times and became known as the "eternal second". Poulidor's rivalry with Jaques Anquetil went deeper than the sports pages: the genial Poulidor was two years Anquetil's junior, and the Norman took a bizarre and cruel pleasure in making sure that his younger rival would never win the Tour. Poulidor rode his last Tour in 1976 at the age of 40, finishing third overall to cap a long Tour career.

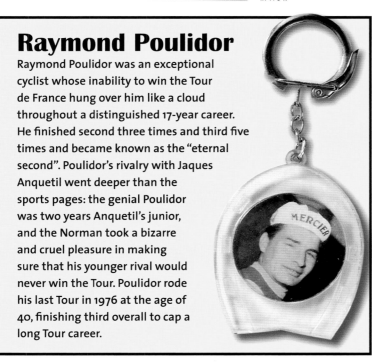

The Merckx Era (1969–1974)

Belgium's first winner of the Tour for 30 years was already
a feared champion before his first victory in 1969. The four that were to follow
confirmed Merckx as a cycling great.

Stage 17, Luchon to Mourenx (214.5km) on Tuesday, 15 July 1969 is remembered as the day Eddy Merckx added his name to the roll of honour of Tour legends. He was already in yellow, having won the team time trial with his Faema squad as well as two individual time trials and two road stages. At the stage start in the Pyrenean town of Luchon, Merckx had an eight-minute advantage over second-placed Roger Pingeon of France, and with only six stages to go he was not expected to do anything other than protect a comfortable overall lead.

Up the mighty Col du Tourmalet, Merckx crossed the top with a slight advantage over Pingeon and Poulidor, while the bunch inched upwards far below. Over the other side Merckx freewheeled, allowing gravity to take effect, his long back flat above his white and red "Eddy Merckx" bike. Down he plummeted, swooping through the corners, enjoying the cooling effect of the wind as the afternoon sun hammered down. On reaching the Pau valley road he knew it was another 18km to the foot of the next climb, the Col du Soulor leading on to the Col d'Aubisque. Merckx was an ace descender but he had no reason to assume that the chasing group would not do everything possible to reel him back in as soon as the road levelled off. He looked behind him. The road was empty, photographers and cameramen astride thudding BMW motorbikes his sole companions as the Belgian once again felt the resistance under his pedals and began to apply greater force.

By the foot of the approach to the Soulor, at Argelès-Gazost, he was over 1-30 ahead of nine chasers. Merckx was climbing easily, with rhythm and power, on a day when he could not "feel the pedals". At the top of the Soulor he had a 4-55 lead, and cresting the Aubisque the advantage was an astonishing seven minutes – unheard of in the modern era. At the line in Mourenx-Ville-Nouvelle the first dejected chasers came in eight minutes behind Merckx. Another seven minutes elapsed before Italian champion Felice Gimondi and 1968 Tour winner Jan Janssen arrived. Merckx had slain the Tour de France beast at his first attempt. In Paris, after Merckx had won the final-stage time trial, the yellow jersey was nearly 18 minutes in front of second-placed Pingeon. No Tour since then has been won by a greater margin.

MERCKX'S WORTHY ADVERSARY

Merckx was peerless again the following year, but a crash during a motor-paced event the previous September, which killed his pacer and injured Merckx's pelvis, gave the Belgian persistent trouble for the rest of his career. The reckless panache of his 1969 Tour win would not be seen again, although that by no means prevented

him from brutally effective exploits such as his stage 14 win on Mont Ventoux which saw Merckx eliminate his main rivals and ensure a second Tour victory.

In 1971, just when the French were growing agitated at the prospect of another Merckx thrashing, a Spaniard named Luis Ocaña put nearly nine minutes into him on the Alpine stage 11 finishing on the climb to Orcières-Merlette. Merckx went on the

TOP: 1971 Tour leader Luis Ocaña's Tour is over as he lies injured on the Col de Mente having been crashed into by Joop Zoetemelk during the torrential rain-hit stage 14

ABOVE: Merckx wins the Pau to Luchon stage of the 1972 Tour. It was one of six stage wins on his way to a fourth Tour victory.

Eddy Merckx

The greatest that ever lived. For once the hyperbole rings true – Eddy Merckx's career record towers over every other great cycling champion. Even Bernard Hinault and Miguel Indurain, who won as many Tours as him, could not match Merckx's all-year-round brilliance. Born on the outskirts of Brussels, the French-speaking Belgian won 445 races in a 13-year career.

Apart from his five Tour wins he also won five Tours of Italy, three world road race championships and no fewer than 32 of the great one-day classics. Not for nothing was he nicknamed "The Cannibal". Merckx retired in 1976 but he has kept close contact through his bicycle company which has supplied "Eddy Merckx" bikes to many teams. His son Axel also had a long career as a pro rider, though without anything like the success of his father.

 **FACTFILE**

Born	17 June 1945, Meensel Kiezegem, Belgium
Team	Peugeot, Faema, Molteni, Fiat
Tour Wins	1969 – 6 stage wins – KoM – points, 1970 – 8 stage wins – KoM, 1971 – 4 stage wins – points, 1972 – 6 stage wins – points, 1974 – 8 stage wins
Other Tours	1975 – 2nd – 2 stage wins, 1977 – 6th

offensive after the rest day, attacking at the start of the long 250km stage 12 to Marseilles but gaining only two minutes on Ocaña at the finish. In the Pyrenees, with time running out for Merckx, both protagonists found themselves descending the Col de Mente in atrocious weather during stage 14. Merckx crashed on a flooded bend, was unhurt and remounted. Soon after, Ocaña also went down, but as he got up Holland's Joop Zoetemelk cannoned into him. Ocaña crumpled, and injuries to his legs and shoulder were enough to put the yellow jersey out of the race there and then. At the finish in Luchon Merckx refused to don the yellow jersey, having inherited the lead – which he held to Paris – thanks to Ocaña's misfortune.

A crash and illness forced Ocaña to pull out of the 1972 Tour and gave "The Cannibal" a trouble-free run to his fourth victory. He scored six stage wins, including the prologue at Angers and the final 42km time trial at Versailles.

OCAÑA'S TOUR

Ocaña finally got his Tour win in 1973, when Merckx stayed away from the Tour having already won the Tours of Spain and Italy beforehand. Ocaña got his bad luck out of the way early on this time – he was brought down by a dog on stage two but got away with superficial grazes. Over the cobbles of northern France the Spaniard infiltrated a break with Cyrille Guimard of France but no other overall favourites. By the finish at Rheims he had two minutes' advantage on Bernard Thévenet, Zoetemelk, Raymond Poulidor and Lucien Van Impe. In the Alps Ocaña saw off the challenge from Spanish climber José Manuel Fuente, and then

60 ans de Tours de France
Par Jean Corhumel
Illustrations d'Alfred Gérard

"Merckx has the head of Bobet, the legs of Coppi, the fitness of Anquetil and the audacity of Koblet."

CYCLING *MAGAZINE*

won three stages in the final eight days to run out a comfortable winner ahead of rising French star Thévenet.

On Merckx's return to the Tour in 1974 his two major rivals, Ocaña and Zoetemelk, were both absent due to contract wrangles and injury. Once again it fell to 38-year-old Poulidor to offer some resistance in the mountain stages. Despite a painful wound on his saddle area after an operation, Merckx was imperious on every terrain, even in the sprints. He won eight stages to advance his Tour total to a new record of 32. On stage 21 from Vouvray to Orléans, Merckx simply rode away from the peloton with 14km to go. Fittingly he won the first leg of a split penultimate stage and the final one, into Paris, to make it five Tour de France wins, equalling the record of Anquetil set ten years before.

Luis Ocaña

Eddy Merckx had many rivals, but Luis Ocaña was one of the few to challenge the Belgian at the height of his career in the Tour de France. Ocaña's stage win to Orcières-Merlette in the 1971 Tour looked set to halt Merckx's bid for a hat-trick of Tour wins, but the Spaniard's crash and exit on the Col de Mente four days later cruelly ended his hopes and snuffed out what could have been one of the greatest contests of the Tour. Ocaña's ten-year career also included one win in his national tour. He was a complex man, driven to avenge the effects of his father's exile from Franco's Spain. He died aged 49, with suicide thought to be the most likely cause.

The Thévenet Era (1975–1977)

France hailed Bernard Thévenet as the David who slew Goliath, also known as Eddy Merckx. Little did they know that this remarkable act of giant-killing would quickly be followed by another.

For the 1975 Tour the organisers introduced a new jersey to be worn by the leader of the mountains classification. The polka dot jersey was white with big red spots and it was worn this year by Lucien Van Impe, the little Belgian who won a total of six King of the Mountains titles. Van Impe was also third overall in the 1975 Tour, but it was the contrasting fortunes of first and second, Bernard Thévenet and Eddy Merckx, that transfixed followers of the 62nd Tour de France.

KING EDDY OVERTHROWN

At the start it was Merckx who looked on course to claim a record-breaking sixth victory. After the 16km stage six time trial around Merlin Plage the Belgian pulled on the yellow jersey, winning at an average speed of more than 30mph (48.28kmh). Thévenet was sixth, nearly a minute down. Merckx won another time trial between Fleurance and Auch, but this time Thévenet was only nine seconds behind over a hilly 37.4km course. The curly-haired Burgundian, riding in Peugeot's distinctive white and chequerboard strip, chipped away at Merckx's lead through the Pyrenees, and on stage 13 to the top of the Puy de Dôme he closed to less than a minute after Merckx was assaulted by a member of the crowd who leapt out and punched him in the stomach.

All was set for a showdown in the Alps, and stage 15 from Nice to Pra Loup did not disappoint. First Merckx took the fight to Thévenet who, after repeated attacks on the Col du Champs, failed to crack King Eddy and instead found himself cast adrift over the summit. Joined by a team-mate, Thévenet called upon all his reserves to rejoin the Merckx group at the foot of the

ABOVE: French veteran Raymond Poulidor in 1976, on the way to his eighth top-three Tour finish without a win.

BELOW: Bernard Thévenet celebrates his shock defeat of Eddy Merckx after stage 15 of the 1975 Tour.

OPPOSITE: Lucien Van Impe rides back into the yellow jersey on the stage to St Lary Soulan during the 1976 Tour.

Col d'Allos, the summit of which was 22.4km from the finish on the climb to Pra Loup. Thévenet lost 15 seconds to Merckx over the top of the Allos, at which point he must have lost hope of toppling the yellow jersey for at least another year. Then on the final ramp to Pra Loup the incredible happened. Merckx suddenly cracked, his elbows appearing to buckle under the weight of his long back as he watched, powerless and unable to react, as the Frenchman caught and passed him without daring to look him in the face.

Bernard Thévenet

Turning professional in 1970, Bernard Thévenet went straight in as one of the leaders of the Peugeot-BP team. In that same year he beat Eddy Merckx, Felice Gimondi and Roger Pingeon in the Mont Faron hill-climb, confirming his exceptional talents as a climber. He finished the Tour de France eight times from ten starts, winning nine stages and, apart from his two wins in 1975 and 1977, was second to Luis Ocaña in 1973. Thévenet retired in 1981 and became a popular and respected commentator on French television.

FACTFILE

Born	10 January 1948, Saint Julien de Civry, France
Team	Peugeot
Tour Wins	1975 – 2 stage wins
	1977 – 1 stage win
Other Tours	1970 – 35th – 1 stage win
	1971 – 4th – 1 stage win
	1972 – 9th – 2 stage wins
	1973 – 2nd – 2 stage wins
	1974 – dnf
	1976 – dnf
	1978 – dnf
	1980 – 17th
	1981 – 37th

FRANCE'S NEW HERO

Thévenet won the stage and pulled on his first yellow jersey. Merckx lost 1-56 but held on to second overall and even closed the gap on Thévenet, despite suffering both from the punch and a subsequent crash which fractured his jaw and meant he could ingest only liquids on the remaining stages to Paris. Thévenet delighted France, but Merckx, in finishing second at 2-47, silenced the moaners with one of his most courageous performances.

A climber won the 1976 Tour. Van Impe was helped by the absence of a fading Merckx, and illness which did for Thévenet in the Pyrenees. Van Impe climbed into the yellow jersey after stage nine from Divonne-les-Bains to L'Alpe d'Huez. He lost it to Frenchman Raymond Delisle a couple of days later, but profited from an attack on stage 14 by 1973 Tour winner Luis Ocaña of Spain on the road to St Lary Soulan, grabbing the opportunity to leave close challenger Zoetemelk behind and retake the yellow jersey. Van Impe held the jersey to Paris and shared the podium with another Belgian, Freddy Maertens, who in his first Tour won eight stages and the green jersey thanks to a ballistic sprint and solo power in short time trials.

A healthy Thévenet came to the 1977 Tour as one of the leading favourites. He had to hurry though, as there was another French champion who had already beaten him in that year's Dauphiné Libéré one-week stage race and although considered too young at 22 for the Tour, was an almost certain contender in 1978. Bernard Hinault did not disappoint and would go on to become a five-times winner. But in 1977 it was a young German wunderkind who stole a march on the field as the race went straight into the Pyrenees on the second day. Dietrich Thurau won the prologue and stage from Auch to Pau and held on to the yellow jersey for a total of 17 days. He lost it after the stage 15 mountain time trial from Morzine to Avoriaz, which was won by Van Impe but promoted Thévenet to yellow. On stage 17 from Chamonix to L'Alpe d'Huez Thévenet was attacked first by Van Impe and then by Dutch all-rounder Hennie Kuiper, who came to within nine seconds of the overall lead at the ski station summit. Van Impe lost nearly two and a half minutes after being struck by a car which threw him off and damaged his back wheel. On the same day Merckx, riding in his last Tour and suffering with dysentery, lost nearly 15 minutes. He still managed to finish sixth overall.

Thévenet had to survive the 50km stage 20 time trial around Dijon, in which Kuiper lost only 28 seconds to him, and the Frenchman arrived in Paris with a slender 48-second advantage to secure his second and final Tour win.

"I passed Merckx without even daring to look at him."

BERNARD THÉVENET, RECALLING STAGE 15 OF THE 1975 TOUR DE FRANCE

OPPOSITE: The moment Merckx "The Cannibal" was eaten alive by Bernard Thévenet (right) on the climb to Pra Loup, stage 15 of the 1975 Tour.

RIGHT: Left to right, Joop Zoetemelk, Bernard Thévenet, Hennie Kuiper and Lucien Van Impe pose for the camera at the end of the 1977 Tour.

LEFT: Joop Zoetemelk takes the stage victory and eventual winner Lucien Van Impe (left) will don the yellow jersey after their attack on L'Alpe d'Huez, stage nine of the 1976 Tour.

THE THÉVENET ERA (1975–1977)

Joop Zoetemelk

Joop Zoetemelk holds the record for the most finishes in the Tour de France. Between 1970 and 1986 he completed 15 Tours, winning one in 1980, and finishing second six times. He missed the 1974 Tour after sustaining a fractured skull in a crash earlier in the season. Like Raymond Poulidor but even more so, Zoetemelk was the "eternal second". The Dutchman rode as a professional for 18 years and had the unique opportunity, or misfortune, to race at the top level against Eddy Merckx and Bernard Hinault. When Hinault abandoned the Tour in 1980, Zoetemelk finally got his Tour win, backed all the way by Dutch superteam Ti-Raleigh. A good one-day rider, Zoetemelk also won the world championship, aged 39, in 1985.

The Hinault Era (1978–1985)

Bernard Hinault's five Tour wins took place at a time when the Tour was entering a period of profound change. It was to his credit and advantage that he embraced it.

Hinault was the last great French champion of the Tour. A proud Breton, he had the strength of character, some would say arrogance, to assume leadership of the tight-knit peloton from an early age. At 23, and riding in his first Tour, he appeared at the head of a riders' protest against overlong transfers, split stages and early starts, his defiant pose at the end of stage 12 in stark contrast to the anxious looks of his colleagues as they stood fumbling with their bikes having climbed off just before the finish line at Valence d'Agen. Hinault was a hot favourite to win the Tour and was roundly abused by press and public for his actions. The French champion knew exactly what he was doing, and this moment set the tone for a career in which he used his immense power and the strength of personality to crush and intimidate his rivals.

He was "Le Patron" (The Boss) during an era when traditional hierarchies were crumbling and deference was giving way to opportunity and ambition. The Tour was changing: in 1982 Phil Anderson became the first Australian to wear the yellow jersey; a year later a team from Colombia opened up the Tour to massive interest from across the Atlantic. Hinault was at the centre of change, with American wonder-kid Greg LeMond a team-mate at La Vie Claire – an international superteam backed by French businessman Bernard Tapie. Hinault was not afraid to embrace change in other ways, and he was the first rider to pioneer the use of the Look ski-binding-type clipless pedals as well as adopting aerodynamic advances in bike technology.

Back in 1978 there was no sign of what was around the corner. Thévenet had won the Tour one year before, but now another young French champion was about to make his Tour debut. His main rivals would be the same riders who had failed to topple Thévenet, Van Impe and even Eddy Merckx. At 36 Joaquim Agostinho had been a professional since 1968 and would finish third overall in the 1978 Tour. He was 41 in the 1983 Tour de France, where he took 11th overall, but died in a racing crash the following year. The Portuguese was no match for Hinault; nor was another Merckx-era rider, Joop Zoetemelk, who was holding the yellow jersey with three days to go but could not hold off Hinault in the long final time trial (72km) from Metz to Nancy, which clinched a debut 1978 Tour victory for the Breton.

SEALING VICTORY IN STYLE

Exactly the same final podium assembled a year later at the end of the 1979 Tour, in which Hinault was imperious in the long time trials and only suffered one hiccup when Zoetemelk put time into into him after a puncture on the cobbled stage to Roubaix. The Tour ended in style when Hinault and Zoetemelk escaped the bunch and duelled for the stage win on the Champs-Elysées. This time the Frenchman made no mistake on the cobbles, putting Zoetemelk firmly in his place with a fairytale stage-winning sprint. As the new decade began, the nearly-man finally got his reward. Zoetemelk profited from Hinault's withdrawal from the Tour with tendinitis while in the yellow jersey on the 12th stage to Pau. The Dutchman and his new Ti-Raleigh team-mates took over the second half of the race, and Zoetemelk earned the win after taking the final time trial at St Etienne.

Four time trials and one mountain stage win confirmed Hinault as the outstanding stage racer of his time when he romped to his third Tour win in 1981. Only Anderson, the first Australian to wear the yellow jersey, looked to have the audacity to challenge the established order. He wore the jersey for one day and finished tenth overall.

"As long as I breathe, I attack."
BERNARD HINAULT

LEFT: Hinault burst on to the 1978 Tour and the old guard of Joop Zoetemelk (in yellow) and Joaquim Agostinho (partly hidden) had no answer to his power and aggression.

Bernard Hinault

Born in Yffiniac, Brittany, Bernard Hinault started out as a junior champion and never looked back. One of the most self-possessed champions, he would set himself a goal and more often than not achieve it and move on. He was famously dismissive of races from the era of the ancients such as Paris–Roubaix, which included many kilometres of cobbled farm tracks. Nevertheless he made a point of winning Paris–Roubaix, just to show that he could, in 1981. Hinault also vowed to retire aged 32 and he did just that, riding his last Tour in 1986 and winning three stages, the King of the Mountains, and lending a hand to Greg LeMond en route to the American's first Tour win.

▬▬ ▭▭ ▬▬ FACTFILE

Born	14 November 1954, Yffiniac, France
Team	Gitane, Renault-Elf-Gitane, La Vie Claire
Tour Wins	1978 – 3 stage wins, 1979 – 7 stages – points, 1981 – 5 stage wins,
Other Tours	1982 – 4 stage wins, 1985 – 3 stage wins
	1980 – dnf – 3 stage wins, 1984 – 2nd – 1 stage win,
	1986 – 2nd – 2 stages – KoM

BELOW: Henri Desgrange was Tour Director from 1903 to 1935. His successor, Jacques Goddet, celebrated his 50th year in charge with a special dinner in 1985.

ABOVE: Hinault won his fourth Tour in 1982 and was so dominant that he outsprinted the entire field to win the final stage on the Champs-Elysées.

L'Auto
AUTOMOBILE – CYCLISME
ATHLÉTISME, YACHTING, AÉROSTATION, ESCRIME, POIDS et HALTÈRES, HIPPISME, GYMNASTIQUE, ALPINISME

LES 50 TOURS DE

L'ÉQUIPE

Samedi 29 Juin 1985
VANNES
dîner
à bord du NAVISPACE

MENU
ASSIETTE DU PÊCHEUR
FILET DE JULIENNE MOUSSELINE
DE MEAUX
CANARD AU VINAIGRE DE CIDRE
GRATIN DAUPHINOIS
FROMAGES
FRAMBOISIER 1929

LES
TROPHÉES PERNOD
sont heureux de vous offrir
PASTIS 51 / PERNOD / SUZE
BYRRH / WHITE HEATHER

Muscadet sur Lie
Saumur Champigny
Café
Champagne

ABOVE: The cult of "The Badger" is celebrated with this record, "Blaireau Reggae".

TOP: Hinault shows off his yellow jerseys after his 1982 triumph.

NEW CHALLENGERS ARISE

Anderson returned in 1982 and held the yellow jersey for ten days after winning stage two to Nancy. No one, however, could match Hinault's formidable time trialling and mastery of the Alps and Pyrenees, and "Le Blaireau" (The Badger) once again relegated Zoetemelk to second overall (his sixth) as he humiliated the peloton by winning the final bunch sprint on the Champs-Elysées.

Just when it looked as if nothing could stop Hinault, a shock result in 1983 was a reminder that nothing in the Tour can be taken for granted. With Hinault once again absent from the race owing to injury, a 23-year-old French first-timer called Laurent Fignon inherited the yellow jersey from his team-mate Pascal Simon, who was unable to continue with a broken shoulder-blade on stage 17 to L'Alpe d'Huez. The bespectacled Fignon won the final time trial at Dijon to cap an astonishing debut win. Fignon showed that his win was no fluke when he returned in the French champion's jersey in 1984 and put Hinault to the sword in the time trials and the mountains. He was particularly impressive in the Alps, winning three stages out of five and taking the yellow jersey after Colombian Luis Herrera's stage win on stage 17 to L'Alpe d'Huez.

Sean Kelly

Sean Kelly won his first green jersey for points in 1982 and went on to win three more in 1983, 1985 and 1989. The Irishman from Carrick-on-Suir was the greatest all-rounder of a group of English-speaking riders from the USA, Australia and the British Isles who in the 1980s changed the face of continental cycling for ever. Kelly's wins included major stage races such as the 1988 Tour of Spain, one-day Classics of every type and short stage races such as Paris–Nice, which he won a record seven times. Famously taciturn, he had a wicked sense of humour and, thanks to his acrobatic skills on the bike, he was able to come up with a technique for making riders scatter in reaction to the sound of a big crash – just by his way of dragging a Coke can along the road.

Hinault's fifth and final Tour de France victory was achieved by a combination of willpower, aggression and mind games. This time it was Fignon who missed the Tour through injury and Hinault was once again favourite. He won the first time trial from Sarrebourg to Strasbourg, taking the yellow jersey, and then made successful attacks in the Alps. But a crash while sprinting to the finish at St Etienne left Hinault with a broken nose that put him on the back foot through the Pyrenees. His young team-mate LeMond had to be persuaded to hold back from taking the lead by his *directeur sportif* Paul Koechli. The cunning Hinault also promised to help the American win the Tour the following year. It worked, and LeMond, despite winning the final time trial around Lac de Vassivière (the first US stage win in Tour history), duly rolled in second overall, just one minute 42 seconds behind Hinault.

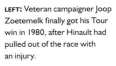

LEFT: Veteran campaigner Joop Zoetemelk finally got his Tour win in 1980, after Hinault had pulled out of the race with an injury.

Modern Times

The Tour de France of the 21st century is a very different event to editions in the 1980s, when the race was not the global phenomenon it is today. The three-week format remains unchanged, however, and it is still the Grand Tour that every champion would love to win. The Tour has not been without its crises in the modern era, foremost of which were the doping scandals of the late 1990s and 2000s.

LEFT: Tours of the modern era have attracted bigger and often rowdier crowds than ever before. Nowhere is that more apparent than on the iconic climb of L'Alpe d'Huez where thousands of Dutch fans add to the party atmosphere.

The LeMond Era (1983–1990)

Greg LeMond was the first American winner of the Tour de France and his duel with Laurent Fignon in the 1989 Tour remains the closest finish in Tour history.

Greg LeMond was one of the first riders to orientate his whole season around winning the Tour de France. The former junior skier turned cyclist had all the attributes of a stage racer: he was a good time triallist and climber and was immensely strong and robust. He also knew that his market value was based on his profile in the USA, where the Tour de France was the only cycle race that received any attention from the general media. Previous champions of the Tour like Eddy Merckx and LeMond's team-mate Bernard Hinault would treat the Tour as one of several season-long objectives. For LeMond it was Le Tour, or nothing.

HINAULT: HELPING OR HINDERING

Having sacrificed the chance to win the race in 1985, when he throttled back to allow an injured Hinault to win his fifth Tour, LeMond came to the 1986 race expecting to have the favour returned by Hinault, who had assured LeMond of his support just months from the Breton's retirement at the end of the same year. "The Badger", either out of sheer devilment or perhaps in the belief that he could snatch a sixth Tour win after all, then proceeded to take the yellow jersey after attacking and leaving LeMond behind on stage 12 from Bayonne to Pau (217.5km) in the Pyrenees. LeMond, stung by Hinault's act of provocation, won the following day's stage from Pau to Superbagnères (186km) and in the Alps overhauled Hinault to take back the yellow jersey after stage 17 from Gap to Le Granon (179.5km). He then joined a runaway Hinault on the descent of the Galibier on stage 18 from Briançon to L'Alpe d'Huez (162.5km), and the two riders rode together up the Alpe, crossing the line with hands clasped high together. Hinault was awarded the stage win and on that day signalled that he would not try again to improve on his second place overall.

LEFT: Stephen Roche became Ireland's first winner of the Tour when he won the 1987 race after a thrilling duel with Pedro Delgado.

BOTTOM: Ceremonial pennant from the 1988 Tour.

OPPOSITE TOP: In 1986 Bernard Hinault was close to retirement but he made his young team-mate Greg LeMond (in yellow) fight for victory virtually all the way to Paris.

OPPOSITE BOTTOM: The 1989 Tour is slipping away from Fignon as he sprints the final metres up the Champs-Elysées.

FACTFILE

Born	26 June 1961, Lakewood, USA
Teams	Renault, La Vie Claire, Z
Tour Wins	1986 – 1 stage win
	1989 – 3 stage wins
	1990 – 0 stage wins
Other Tours	1984 – 3rd
	1985 – 2nd – 1 stage win
	1991 – 7th
	1992 – dnf
	1994 – dnf

Greg LeMond

Had it not been for the hunting accident in 1987, Greg LeMond looked set to continue winning the Tour de France in the years following his first victory in 1986. Five Tour wins would not have been unrealistic for the Californian, who understood very well the rewards that Tour success could bring during the globalisation of the sport in the 1980s. LeMond was a pioneer of cycling equipment such as the triathlon bars, aero helmet and lightweight racing sunglasses. He also signed the first million-dollar contract, for $5.5m over three years with the "Z" team in 1989. Another race also motivated LeMond – he won the world road race championship twice, in 1983 and 1989.

77

78

SEESAW TOURS

No one knew who would win the 1987 Tour, as LeMond was recovering from shotgun wounds sustained in a hunting accident that would keep him out of the Tour for two years. Ten years later another American, Lance Armstrong, would also sit out the Tour for two years before returning, free from cancer, though his first and six subsequent wins were all later withdrawn. Hinault had retired and Fignon was not in Tour-winning form. Berlin hosted the prologue; it was the furthest from France that the Tour had ever been for a Grand Départ, and an open race lived up to its name with the yellow jersey constantly changing hands. In all the race surpassed the previous record with eight different riders wearing the yellow jersey, and it was not until the stage 18 time trial from Carpentras to Mont Ventoux (36.5km) that a credible winner emerged in the classy Frenchman Jean-François Bernard. An untimely puncture ended his hopes the next day as the two final protagonists of the 1987 race, Ireland's Stephen Roche and Pedro Delgado of Spain, engaged in a thrilling scrap for the lead which played out in the Irishman's favour after he had heroically pegged back Delgado's lead on the stage 21 finish to La Plagne. Roche stole back some seconds the following day, out-descending Delgado off the Joux Plane, and in the final stage 24 time trial around Dijon he regained the overall lead with only the triumphant ride into Paris to come.

Delgado got his Tour win in 1988. Roche was out with injury and the Spaniard rode into yellow on stage 12 to L'Alpe d'Huez, consolidating his lead a day later in the time trial from Grenoble

ABOVE: After the closest ever Tour finish in 1989, winner Greg LeMond is all smiles while runner-up Laurent Fignon muses on what might have been.

"Greg believes he can win. But it is impossible. I am too strong in the mind and the legs. Fifty seconds is too much to make up in such a short distance."

LAURENT FIGNON, BEFORE FINAL TT 1989 TOUR

Laurent Fignon

Born in Paris and a graduate of veterinary science, the bespectacled Laurent Fignon did not fit the mould of a typical professional cyclist. However, his two Tour de France victories, as well as one Tour of Italy and two Milan–San Remo Classic wins in his 11-year career mark out "The Professor" as one of the most versatile and exciting riders of the 1980s. His eight-second defeat at the hands of LeMond at the end of the 1989 Tour was such a dramatic and emotional moment in his career that he will always be remembered as the man who lost the Tour in the space of a few hundred metres on the Champs-Elysées.

to Villard de Lans (38km). From there to Paris he was troubled only by a dope test which showed traces of a substance that was not on the banned list, but was known as a masking agent for steroids.

LeMond's return to the Tour and a resurgent Fignon resulted in the closest Tour finish in history at the end of the 1989 race. Delgado might also have played a part in the fight for the lead had he not started over two minutes late in the prologue and then lost more time on the first road stage in Luxembourg city. Fighting back over the remaining three weeks he eventually finished third at 3-34 to LeMond. The American and the pony-tailed Frenchman swapped the lead in the middle of the race with just seconds separating them. By stage 17 from Briançon to L'Alpe d'Huez, however, Fignon regained the lead and went into the final stage 21 time trial in the centre of Paris with a 50-second advantage over LeMond. Then, making full use of a new aerodynamic bar which placed both arms together in a ski-style tuck, LeMond recorded the fastest Tour time trial average speed to wipe out Fignon's lead and finish the winner by just eight seconds.

Riding for the French "Z" team, LeMond returned in 1990 to win his third Tour with relative ease. He took the jersey with just one day left to race after a three-week war of attrition on three members of a four-man break who had gained 10-35 on stage one around Futuroscope (138.5km). All three took turns in the yellow jersey: Steve Bauer of Canada wore it until the Alps, then Ronan Pensec of France held it for two days before Italian Claudio Chiappucci inherited the lead with the Pyrenees to come. The

feisty Italian rode with great courage and panache to hang on to a slender lead through the Pyrenees, but he could do nothing about LeMond in the final stage 20 time trial around Lac de Vassivière, where the American easily overcame a five-second deficit. LeMond took yellow and rode up the Champs-Elysées the next day to record his third Tour win without having won a single stage.

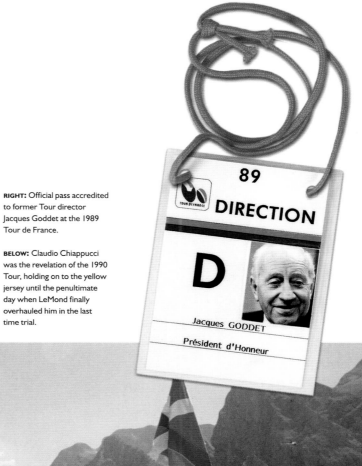

RIGHT: Official pass accredited to former Tour director Jacques Goddet at the 1989 Tour de France.

BELOW: Claudio Chiappucci was the revelation of the 1990 Tour, holding on to the yellow jersey until the penultimate day when LeMond finally overhauled him in the last time trial.

The Indurain Era (1991–1998)

Five consecutive Tour wins: no one had ever achieved such a feat before Miguel Indurain began his unassailable winning run in 1991.

Sports fans in the USA discovered the Tour through Greg LeMond, who was the first American cyclist of the modern era to earn widespread acclaim in a European sport that hitherto had barely registered on the US sports radar. During the 1980s the Tour had also begun to open up to nations from around the globe, with a team of amateur riders from Colombia invited in 1983, the increasingly frequent successes of English-speaking riders such as Phil Anderson and Sean Kelly, and then the impact of eastern bloc riders from 1990 on. By the time the 1991 Tour was held, the race was a truly international event. Stage winners this year apart from the established cycling nations included riders from Brazil, Uzbekistan, Australia and Russia. Uzbek Djamolidine Abdoujaparov also became the first East European to win the green points jersey.

None, however, had any answer to a statuesque rider from Spain who, in his sixth Tour, stepped up and calmly demolished every other overall contender. Miguel Indurain was no shooting star across the cycling firmament. He came to the 1991

prologue in Lyons honed and chiselled into a Tour-winning machine, having already completed four of six Tours entered with placings of 97th, 47th, 17th and 10th. The man from Villava on the edge of Pamplona in northern Spain had ridden loyally in the service of Pedro Delgado, winner in 1988, and under the acute eye of his Banesto team *directeur sportif* José Miguel Echavarri he was now ready, at 26, to take on the responsibility of being a Tour contender.

PEERLESS POWER

It was to prove a Tour too far for LeMond, who started as a favourite and even held the yellow jersey after finishing second to Indurain in the stage eight time trial from Argentan to Alençon (73km). In the Pyrenees he could not match the pace of Indurain, who picked up Claudio Chiappucci, the revelation of the 1990 Tour, and pedalled inexorably away from the field on stage 13 from Jaca to the summit finish of Val Louron. Chiappucci won the stage and would go on to win the King of

ABOVE: Souvenir badge from the 1994 Tour.

RIGHT: Indurain leads, Tony Rominger follows. The Spaniard's closest rival became accustomed to the sight of the yellow jersey on the broad shoulders of "Big Mig".

OPPOSITE: Indurain was the consummate time triallist.

ABOVE: Miguel Indurain's Pinarello in 1995 was the height of aerodynamic fashion.

"A man of amazing physiological capacities, his resting heart-rate was 28 beats per minute, his pulmonary capacity more than eight litres and his pedalling power nearly 600 watts."

JEAN-PAUL OLLIVIER ON MIGUEL INDURAIN

Miguel Indurain

Miguel Indurain is the greatest Spanish champion of the Tour with five outright victories, 12 stage wins and a total of 60 days in the yellow jersey. He was the first rider to win five consecutive Tours. One curious aspect to his Tour wins is that he never managed to win a massed-start stage from 1991 to 1995. Indurain did not always treat the Tour as his sole annual objective – he also won the Tour of Italy twice and was a strong performer in the world road race championship, winning a bronze and two silvers. After 99 wins as a professional, Indurain retired with his family near to his home town of Villava and the farm where he was brought up. Modest to the point of anonymity, Indurain has maintained loose contact with cycling through his involvement with the Spanish Olympic Committee and the UCI's Professional Cycling Council.

FACTFILE

Born	16 July 1964, Villava, Spain
Team	Banesto
Tour Wins	1991 – 2 stage wins, 1992 – 3 stage wins, 1993 – 2 stage wins, 1994 – stage win, 1995 – 2 stage wins
Other Tours	1985 – dnf, 1986 – dhf, 1987 – 97th, 1988 – 47th, 1989 – 17th – 1 stage win, 1990 – 10th – 1 stage win, 1996 – 11th

the Mountains prize and finish third overall. Indurain pulled on the yellow jersey, held Italian Gianni Bugno at 3-36 in second place and won the final stage 21 time trial from Lugny to Macon (57km) en route to the first of five Tour wins.

Awesome power in the time trials and crushing consistency in the mountains was Indurain's method and it worked every time. In 1992 Chiappucci and Bugno swapped places on the podium but the top step was once again occupied by the Spaniard, who won the prologue in San Sebastian, time trial stages in Luxembourg (65km) and Tours-Blois (64km) and climbed into the overall lead after an epic stage 13 to Sestriere. This Alpine stage was the scene of Chiappucci's greatest exploit as the pugnacious Italian embarked on a 125km breakaway which landed him the stage win and guaranteed second place in Paris. Behind, Indurain contained Chiappucci, inheriting yellow and wearing it from there to the finish.

A strong challenger to Indurain's reign emerged in 1993 in the form of Switzerland's Tony Rominger, who could climb and time trial. He would have his work cut out, as "Miguelon" was at the height of his powers, having just won the Tour of Italy for the second year running and looking to create a new record by doing the Giro-Tour double in consecutive years. Indurain was again unbeatable in the prologue around Le Puy de Fou and predictably took the yellow jersey after the stage nine time trial around Lac de Madine (59km). Rominger responded with back-to-back stage wins in the Alps, but the metronomic Indurain kept him pegged at all times. Rominger's victory in the

stage 19 time trial from Bretigny-sur-Orge to Monthléry (48km) came too late to trouble the leader, but it raised hopes for a tighter contest in 1994.

But there was no reduction in Indurain's powers in the next two tours. These followed the same pattern as before, with time trial wins and suffocating rides in the Alps and Pyrenees that none of his rivals could withstand. In 1994 the Tour visited England for the second time in its history, and during the race both Chris Boardman, the prologue winner in Lille, and super-*domestique* Sean Yates wore the yellow jersey for short spells. Another Swiss rider took over from Rominger in the 1995 Tour, but Alex Zülle could do nothing about Indurain, who took the lead after the stage eight time trial from Huy to Seraing (54km), one day after tearing away from the field on the Côte des Forges with Johan Bruyneel of Belgium. The death of Italian Olympic champion Fabio Casartelli, who sustained a fatal head injury after crashing on the descent of the Portet d'Aspet, cast a shadow over the final week.

A Dane, Bjarne Riis, finished third overall in the 1995 Tour and returned with a new team, Telekom, convinced that he could topple Indurain in 1996. With a young German, Jan Ullrich, at his side he delivered the killer blow that brought the Indurain era to an end in a matter of days. Through the Alps on a shortened 46km stage nine to Sestriere, Indurain had no answer to the pace set by Riis, who grabbed the yellow jersey after dropping Russian race leader Evgeni Berzin. On stage 16, to Hautacam, Riis was imperious as he out-climbed all the

specialists and staked a strong claim to victory in Paris. His progress to the finish was only interrupted by the 22-year-old Ullrich's win on the stage 20 Bordeaux to St Emilion time trial which brought him to within 1-41 of Riis.

A FIRST FOR GERMANY

It would not be long before Ullrich succeeded his captain, and on stage 10 from Luchon to Arcalis (252.5km) the following year he dropped the Dane and everyone else to take a decisive win and the overall lead from Richard Virenque of France. Virenque pushed Ullrich all the way to Paris, but he could never match Ullrich against the watch and in the end finished a distant 9-09 behind.

Joining Ullrich and Virenque on the podium of the 1997 Tour was a pure climber from the heroic school of cycling. Marco Pantani had won two mountain stages in the Tour to add to the two he had won in 1995. In 1998, during a Tour almost wrecked by the Festina doping scandal, police raids on hotels, rider strikes and the defection of six teams, Pantani waited until stage 15 from Grenoble to Les Deux Alpes (189km) to launch his bid for victory. In pouring rain Ullrich, in yellow,

Claudio Chiappucci

Claudio Chiappucci's 14-year career took off at the 1990 Tour de France when, ranked as a mere *domestique* or team helper, he tenaciously wore the yellow jersey during the final week and finished second overall to Greg LeMond. The man from Varese would never win the Tour, but in the years that followed he won the mountains prize twice and was a three-time best climber in the Tour of Italy. A prolific racer, he also competed at the off-road discipline of cyclo-cross in the winter off-season. Chiappucci's victory in the 1991 Milan–San Remo early-season Classic was his finest one-day result. In the Tour he was also third overall in 1991, second in 1992 and sixth in 1993.

cracked on the final climb, allowing the Italian to escape to win the stage and claim the overall lead. Ullrich won the stage 20 time trial from Montceaux-les-Mines to Le Creusot (52km), but an inspired Pantani held him at bay to win a torrid 85th edition of the race.

OPPOSITE: Jan Ullrich became Germany's first winner of the Tour de France in 1997, ending more than nine minutes ahead of runner-up Richard Virenque.

LEFT: In 1996 Bjarne Riis put an end to the Indurain era after cracking the five-time winner in the Alps.

BELOW: Souvenir Tour de France medal.

THE INDURAIN ERA (1991–1998)

The Armstrong Era (1999–2005)

Lance Armstrong's recovery from cancer was a feel-good story for cycling in the late 1990s, when the sport was hit with a series of doping scandals. The Texan was in a position to change cycling; instead he drove it deeper into crisis at the start of the millennium.

Lance Armstrong had the chance to be a cycling hero and when he made a miraculous comeback from cancer his many fans in cycling and general public warmed to his story. Fervently wishing for a clean era after the scandals of Pantani and 1998, the Texan cynically exploited the sport of cycling while racking up Tour wins.

A combination of ruthless dominance in the mountains and time trials and robotic teamwork from his US Postal squad helped to bring Armstrong seven consecutive overall Tour victories from 1999 to 2005, an unbelievable record that many followers of cycling found profoundly suspicious.

Sure enough, seven years after his final victory, Armstrong was

stripped of his Tour titles as evidence from his national anti-doping agency revealed him to be a long-time user and trafficker of banned doping products and the man at the heart of US Postal's complicit in-team doping network. A miraculous success story become one of sport's great frauds, albeit in an era where few Tour stars emerged untainted.

Armstrong owed everything to the Tour and to cancer, as it was his recovery from testicular cancer prior to his first Tour win in 1999 that propelled his name far beyond the sports bulletins. Treatment throughout 1997, with few positive signs that he would recover, led many to believe that Armstrong's fledgling career would end in tragedy. But 1998 witnessed a remarkable comeback with a new team, US Postal, and a late-season fourth place in the three-week Tour of Spain.

FIRST WIN
Armstrong won the prologue time trial at Le Puy de Fou, but it was still too early to predict how the 1999 Tour would unfold. At the time, the main sentiment was one of relief that a rider untainted by the doping revelations that nearly sunk the 1998 Tour was the first wearer of the yellow jersey in this so-called "Tour of Redemption". When Armstrong won again in the important first time trial at Metz, and two days later hit them again with victory at the summit of the Sestriere ski resort in the Italian Alps, the comeback, the miracle, was as real as could be.

In 1999 Armstrong won four stages and the overall. In 2000 he won a single stage, the time trial at Mulhouse, and although he once again used his fast pedalling technique to out-climb his rivals and take the yellow jersey on the road to Hautacam, he lost time to Ullrich on the Joux Plane and slipped up when he ushered Pantani across the line ahead of him to take the prestigious stage on Mont Ventoux. The Italian did not appreciate the gesture and said so. Armstrong was stung. He would not make the same mistake again.

"Lance Armstrong has no place in cycling. He deserves to be forgotten... Something like this must never happen again."

UCI PRESIDENT PAT MCQUAID, 2012

ABOVE LEFT: Lance Armstrong in pursuit of his rival Fernando Escartin on stage 16 of the 1999 Tour.

LEFT: Armstrong and Joseba Belokl ride in the middle of the pack during stage eight of the 2002 Tour de France.

1903•2003

CENTENAIRE DU TOUR DE FRANCE

le TOUR de France

DU 5 AU 27 JUILLET 2003

TOP LEFT: Lance Armstrong struggles through the middle section of stage eight in the 2003 Tour.

ABOVE: This special official poster was produced to celebrate the 100th anniversary of the Tour de France.

Armstrong's downfall

A federal investigation into allegations of doping was opened in mid 2010, partly following claims from ex-team-mate and stripped 2006 winner Floyd Landis. Ex-team-mates and staff were subpoenaed into testifying before the investigation was unexpectedly closed in February 2012. The US Anti-Doping Agency then compiled evidence, with more than a dozen ex-team-mates and backroom staff providing testimony. The result was comprehensive, compelling evidence of Armstrong's guilt as a user and trafficker of banned doping products as part of a US Postal conspiracy. In October 2012, Armstrong was officially stripped of his seven Tour titles by cycling's governing body and dropped by a host of lucrative backers. In a nod to the widespread nature of the cheating in his era, his seven Tour wins have been left blank in the record books and not assigned to others.

FACTFILE

Born	18 September 1971, Plano, USA
Teams	Radio Shack, Astana, Discovery, US Postal
Tour Wins	In the seven Tours 1999–2005, Armstrong won 4, 1, 4, 4, 1, 5 and 1 stages, respectively. However, he was stripped of all his stage and seven Tour wins in 2012
Other Tours	1993 – dnf – 1 stage win, 1995 – 36th – 1 stage win, 2009 – 3rd, 2010 – 23rd

Win number three put right the miscalculations of the year before. Ullrich was crushed by four Armstrong stage wins, and the Texan even had time to refine his racecraft, with a killer stare that withered his opponents on L'Alpe d'Huez.

Ullrich's no-show because of injury allowed Spaniard Joseba Beloki to take second place to Armstrong in 2002. Four stage wins, including the prologue and the first mountain stage to La Mongie in the Pyrenees, put the yellow jersey on his back, and victory the next day to Plateau de Beille cemented the advantage. At 30 years old Armstrong's fourth Tour win put him one step away from the all-time Tour de France greats with five wins: Anquetil, Merckx, Hinault and Indurain.

Just over a minute separated Armstrong from Ullrich at the finish of the 2003 Tour – the closest contest of the Armstrong era and a suitably epic race to celebrate his record-equalling fifth Tour win. The 2003 Tour had it all: Armstrong running on empty in the first time trial; his off-road excursion to avoid Beloki in the Alps; his tangle with a spectator and stage win at Luz Ardiden; and Ullrich's agonising crash in the rain during the final time trial to Nantes. Armstrong joined Club Five with a ride that showed him at his combative best.

OUT OF THIS WORLD

No man had ever won more than five Tours, but Armstrong broke the record in 2004 with his most dominating display yet, winning five stages and relegating Ullrich to an also-ran.

Business ties with his team and the arrival of a new sponsor in Discovery Channel TV was enough to get him to line up for the 2005 Tour. The American took one stage win, the final time trial, in a Tour that he approached with less fire in his belly than in previous years. It would be his last before retirement.

Armstrong made a surprise return to the sport three years later for another shot at the Tour. Part of the Astana team, he finished third in the 2009 Tour, outpaced and outfoxed by younger team-mate Alberto Contador. Although Armstrong retired for good at the beginning of 2011, his past, doing what many of his Tour rivals could never do, caught up with him to end one the ugliest eras in cycling history.

ABOVE: Armstrong (in yellow) and Iban Mayo fall on Luz Ardiden during the 2003 Tour. Jan Ullrich (in green) waited for the Texan to rejoin, then lost the stage to him.

RIGHT: The 2005 Tour was Armstrong's last for four years – he eventually made his return with Astana in 2009.

OPPOSITE: Armstrong's story was the stuff of sporting fairy tales, but his relationship with cycling, and with the press, would break down as details of his actions came to light.

BELOW: Jan Ullrich of Germany was another of the high-profile names caught up in a doping scandal..

Jan Ullrich

The former East German, who won the Tour in 1997 aged just 23, could hardly have anticipated that his winning run at the Tour would be so short. Thanks to the Armstrong era Ullrich was destined to finish runner-up to the Texan on three occasions. He was also second to Riis in 1996 and to Pantani in 1998. Ullrich's incredible natural talent made him a formidable adversary to Armstrong. "Der Kaiser" was capable of winning world time trial titles, the Olympic road race and a Tour of Spain but his notorious lack of focus in the off-season often resulted in frantic efforts to lose weight and hit form every July. Ullrich's career ended in disgrace when he was withdrawn from the start of the 2006 Tour after being implicated in a Spanish blood doping ring. He never raced again and was partly to blame for T-Mobile's exit from cycling sponsorship in 2007.

The Years of Zero Tolerance (2006–2008)

After two years rocked by scandal, the Tour hit back in determined manner in 2008, excluding the team of the defending champion and running the race under French rules.

If the 95th Tour de France of 2008 was hoping to make headlines by not inviting 2007 Tour winner Alberto Contador and his Astana team, it certainly succeeded. Still smarting from the blood doping positives posted by Astana's Alexandre Vinokourov and Andrei Kashechkin during and after the 2007 race, the shock announcement that Astana would not be invited to the 2008 edition sent a powerful anti-doping message through the sport.

Few mourned the loss to cycling of the disgraced Kazakh riders but there was consternation that the 2007 Tour winner Alberto Contador would not get the chance to defend his title. Contador had won the Tour riding for the Discovery team but when the US TV channel withdrew its sponsorship, the Johan Bruyneel-run squad was invited by Astana to step in and do whatever it took to rehabilitate the benighted squad. The 24-year-old Spaniard elected to stay with Bruyneel and signed for Astana, expecting to receive the same peerless levels of support in the quest for his second Tour win. Bruyneel's Astana would in effect be the same outfit that had supported Lance Armstrong throughout his seven-year Tour victory run.

Contador had inherited the yellow jersey with four days remaining of the 2007 race after race leader Michael Rasmussen was sensationally withdrawn from his Rabobank team. The Dane had lied about his whereabouts in the run-up to the 2007 race,

evading his pre-competition dope controls and effectively earning the same punishment as for a positive test.

Rasmussen's chicanery was the final embarrassing incident of the 2007 Tour and the French response in 2008 was to say *non* to Astana and Contador. It was pointed out that Bruyneel had instigated an internal anti-doping programme that included blood profiling as followed by leading "clean" teams CSC and Slipstream. There were also other teams which had shamed the 2007 Tour: T-Mobile, Cofidis and Saunier Duval. None was excluded from the 2008 race. But the point had been made and, however inconsistent, it marked another step on cycling's painful road to redemption.

As momentous as the exclusion of Astana was the Tour's decision to break all ties with the world governing body, the Union Cycliste International (UCI), and bring in officials from the French federation to run the race under national rules. The rift with the UCI was largely due to a long-running wrangle over the ProTour series. This was to be the year that the UCI's troubled super-league of teams and races finally fizzled out, and it was the Tour's

BELOW: British super-sprinter Mark Cavendish celebrates his third stage win in the 2008 Tour – Stage 12 into Narbonne.

BOTTOM: Guest's wristband from the party in the tented village in London's Hyde Park on the day of the 2007 Tour Prologue.

London 2007

London and the south-east of England turned out in massive numbers to greet the 2007 Tour as it made only its third visit to the UK. An estimated two million people lined the 7.9km prologue route in central London and one million came out for the 203km stage one from London to Canterbury the following day, as sunshine and blue skies miraculously broke through after a wet and dismal summer. British riders Bradley Wiggins and David Millar failed to win the prologue and young GB sprint hope Mark Cavendish crashed out of the finale of the first stage to Canterbury, but the race was a massive success and hailed by the Tour as the best Grand Départ in recent history. The celebratory start of the 94th Tour was in stark contrast to the previous year's edition, which took place under a cloud following the pre-race withdrawal of race favourites Jan Ullrich and Ivan Basso, both implicated in the Operacion Puerto drugs investigation. The aftermath of the 2006 Tour was no better, with winner Floyd Landis testing positive for testosterone and overall victory handed to runner-up Oscar Pereiro of Spain.

LEFT: Alberto Condador, Tour winner in 2007, sat out the 2008 Tour while his Astana team was punished for dragging the Tour through the mud.

BOTTOM LEFT: Poster celebrating London's hosting of the Grand Départ in 2007.

BELOW: Poster designers have to be inventive when they create the images for each Tour and in 2008 it was kept simple: France's love affair with the bicycle and cycling.

ABOVE: On L'Alpe d'Huez Cadel Evans and Frank Schleck (in yellow) were bested by Carlos Sastre.

rejection of all UCI influence on itself that hammered home the last nail in the original ProTour concept.

Even without Contador there was an air of nervous excitement as the great entourage converged on Brittany for a tradition-breaking first stage of the race from Brest to Plumelec. This was the first time that the Tour had not started with a prologue time trial since 1967 and the prospect of the whole pack fighting for the first yellow jersey of the race was a tantalising prospect. Another innovation which the Tour hoped would liven up the stages was a race radio blackout for the first 50km of every stage. If the *directeurs sportifs* sitting in team cars behind the race could not communicate with their teams via their earpieces, the Tour reasoned that race-enlivening breakaways might stand a better chance of staying clear.

CAVENDISH SPRINTS TO PROMINENCE

It worked, up to a point, but the sprinters still took the lion's share of the wins on the flat stages with Mark Cavendish, 23, the standout performer taking four big bunch stage wins in the first

"This has to change now. The re-conquering of cycling has to be done with the Tour de France."
CHRISTIAN PRUDHOMME

two weeks. The only British rider to win more than one stage in a Tour was Barry Hoban in both 1969 and 1973. Hoban's long-standing outright GB record of eight stage wins (the last one in 1974) had been halved in one Tour, but the Isle of Man-based Briton was already a big star on the world stage, as only the greatest sprint champions have ever won four stages in a single Tour.

Cavendish's wins, French successes, which included three stage wins, and enthusiastic crowds as the race headed south through the centre of France to the Pyrenees, before the sun-kissed easterly trek to the Alps, gave the race an air of confidence and optimism. It was a feelgood factor that positive dope tests failed to dislodge. There were four positives during the race and one team, Saunier

Carlos Sastre

In his tenth year as a professional, Carlos Sastre was one of the few veterans of the peloton to have come through ten turbulent years of the sport untouched by scandal yet still in a position to win the Tour. A four-time top-ten finisher of the Tour with best placings of third in 2006 and fourth in 2007, Sastre's victory in the 2008 race was based on a successful attack on Alpe d'Huez, above average performances in the two short time trials and his all-powerful CSC team. Sastre won the Tour just in time – his young team-mate Andy Schleck was being groomed for team leadership and Sastre must have known that his position at CSC was untenable when he announced two months after the Tour that he was joining the new Cervelo TestTeam. Sastre's move was noteworthy. The announcement shortly after that Lance Armstrong was back in training, aged 36, and targeting a possible eighth Tour win, sent the cycling world into a frenzy that overshadowed everything else.

Duval, went home in disgrace after their team leader Riccardo Ricco tested positive for a new form of the blood-boosting drug EPO. Ricco was caught using a new test being used by L'Agence Française de Lutte Contre le Dopage (French anti-doping agency) and this was seen as another timely reminder that the sport was resolute in cutting out the cheats. Just as damaging, however, were the positive tests announced in the autumn of double time trial stage winner Stefan Schumacher, Bernard Kohl, third overall and King of the Mountains winner, and Leonardo Piepoli.

RIGHT: Carlos Sastre wins Stage 17 in 2008.

LEFT: Coin minted for the 2007 race, with the Tour logo on one side and the map of La Grand Boucle on the other.

ABOVE: Carlos Sastre celebrates his 2008 Tour victory in Paris, accompanied by his two children.

CLOSE BATTLE

What also helped to divert attention from the expulsions during the 2008 Tour was the battle for the yellow jersey, which was as close as it had ever been and with just six days to go, there were six riders all within 49 seconds of leading the race. They had already been to Italy, to finish stage 15 at the 1500-metre summit of Prato Nevoso, and it was here that pre-race favourite Cadel Evans handed over yellow to Luxembourg's Frank Schleck of the formidable team CSC.

Coming back to France on stage 16 the race crossed the highest climb ever ridden in the Tour and the highest road in France, the 2802-metre-high Cime de la Bonette. Visited only four times in the race's history, the high-speed descent from the Bonette caught out two of the six overall contenders when Christian Vande Velde and Denis Menchov both lost time through crashes and getting dropped.

Stage 17, the final day in the Alps and the fourth and final summit finish, was to be the 25th visit by the Tour to L'Alpe d'Huez and as always, the stage did not disappoint. While brothers Frank and Andy Schleck of CSC marked the favourites, their Spanish team-mate Carlos Sastre went clear on the 21-hairpin bend ascent and rode into yellow with a 1-34 lead over Evans. The Australian had been suffering from the effects of a big crash in the Pyrenees and with none of his Silence–Lotto team-mates to help with the chase he lost precious time on Sastre which he could only now attempt to wipe out in the final 53km time trial.

It was not to be, and while Evans rode well enough to jump from fourth overall to second, he could not close to more than 1-05 on Sastre, blowing the biggest opportunity yet for a historic first Tour win by an Australian. The following day Sastre, 33, swept into Paris as a worthy victor of the 95th Tour. The quiet man of Spanish cycling was a popular and suitably humble winner of a Tour, which reasserted itself by celebrating longevity, beauty and culture some way above the worship of brittle heroes.

Worlds Collide (2009–2012)

Two countries celebrated first winners of the Tour in 2011 and 2012. First Cadel Evans of Australia became the oldest post-World War 2 winner, then Great Britain celebrated Sir Bradley Wiggins's and Team Sky's domination.

MODERN TIMES

In 2010 Alberto Contador "won" his third Tour de France largely thanks to a mechanical mishap which befell his main rival Andy Schleck of Luxembourg. Attacking on stage 15's climb of the Port de Balès, Schleck was riding away from Contador when his chain came off as he shifted into a higher gear.

As the hovering TV helicopter relayed a scene of high drama, the yellow jersey-wearing Schleck came to an abrupt halt in the middle of the pass as he desperately tried to put his chain back on. Contador, who was already reacting to Schleck's attack, pounced without a second glance. While viewers debated the ethics of attacking a yellow jersey tripped up by a malfunctioning bike, Contador showed the world why he was the most ruthless grand tour rider in the post-Lance Armstrong comeback era. Riding hard all the way to the finish in Bagnères de Luchon Contador took enough time out of Schleck to wrest the yellow jersey from him.

With five stages of the 2010 Tour to go, Contador's day of luck and opportunism won him a lead of 39 seconds over Andy Schleck. In Paris, after Mark Cavendish had taken his fifth stage win of the race and become the first rider to take consecutive sprint wins on the Champs-Elysées, the Spaniard mounted the final podium with the same 39-second margin gained on that fateful stage 15.

It seemed that this was Contador's third Tour de France victory in as many starts. Dominant in 2007 and 2009, he sat out the race in 2008 when his team, Astana, was excluded after positive tests on two of its riders the previous year. A magnet for controversy, Contador then found himself as a team-mate to the 37-year-old Lance Armstrong in his comeback year in 2008. Armstrong, after a four-year break from pro cycling, would finish an astonishing third overall having frequently blind-sided an angry Contador during the race.

Contador's only challengers in the Alps, the Schleck brothers, tried but failed to gain time on him. Contador won the final stage 18 time trial at Annecy and on stage 20's much anticipated final showdown on Mont Ventoux, he neutralised every attempt to drop him on the barren "Giant of Provence". The following day belonged to Contador, whose triumphant arrival on the Champs-Elysées confirmed him as the first rider capable of making a serious assault on Armstrong's seven Tour wins.

"It's been one of the cleanest Tours in a long, long time."

PAT McQUAID, UCI PRESIDENT, 2011

ABOVE: Alberto Contador (in the polka dot juersey) and Lance Armstrong formed an uneasy alliance as Astana team-mates in 2009.

BELOW: Andy Schleck was awarded the 2010 Tour de France after Alberto Contador had been stripped of the title.

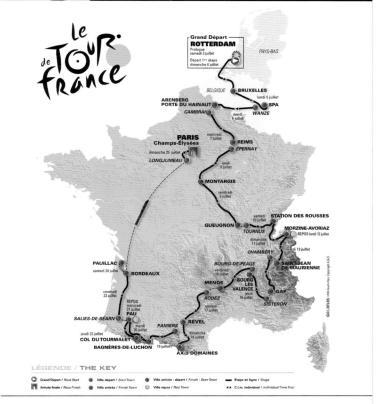

ABOVE LEFT: Spain featured in the 2009 Tour with a stage start and finish in Barcelona.

ABOVE: The 2010 Tour Grand Départ returned to the Netherlands and visited the capital of Belgium en route to France.

STRIPPED OF VICTORY

Two years later and another storm crashed around Contador's head as, following his third Tour win in 2010, a positive test during the race for Clenbuterol dragged on up to and beyond the 2011 Tour. In February 2012, he was stripped of the Tour victory and suspended by the Court of Arbitration for Sport, with Andy Schleck being promoted to winner.

Hollywood could not have scripted it better when, on the first stage of the 2011 race, Contador was held up by a mass pile-up and lost 1-20 to the leading overall contenders. From then on the 98th Tour was set fair to become a vintage edition as the embattled champion played catch-up in an enthralling race won by Cadel Evans. The Australian made history as the first ever Aussie winner of the Tour and his dogged nearly-man status made him one of the most popular Tour victors of modern times.

But before Evans took centre stage in a final time trial in which he overturned a 54-second deficit on Andy Schleck, the Tour was sizzling along nicely with, at last, a credible French yellow jersey. Thomas Voeckler took the yellow jersey after stage nine to Saint-Flour and then heroically proceeded to hang with the best climbers on stage 12 to Luz Ardiden. Repelling

attacks from Evans, the Schlecks, Samuel Sanchez and Contador, French fans dared to hope that after a hiatus of 26 years, one of their own might win the Tour. Voeckler had other ideas – he knew the mountains would eventually crack him and that a great time triallist he was not. Nevertheless he relinquished the jersey only on stage 19 to L'Alpe d'Huez, after encouraging his Europcar team-mate Pierre Rolland to become only the second Frenchman to win on the Alpe after Bernard Hinault in 1986.

All the while Evans lurked in the top three overall, avoiding the crashes of a nervous first week, motivating team BMC to second in the stage two team time trial and always finishing within seconds of the best climbers in the Pyrenees and Alps. Andy Schleck, the younger brother of Frank, put in a suicidal attack on the Col d'Izoard 60km from the summit finish on Col du Galibier in stage 18, knowing that he needed a big chunk of time to have any chance of holding off Evans in the stage 20 time trial. At the bottom of the 2,645-metre-high Galibier Schleck had a race-winning four-minute advantage over

Evans. The Australian won the Tour over the next 23km uphill, relentlessly chomping into Andy's lead as the Luxemburger began to wilt on the highest climb of the 2011 Tour.

At the top, the gap between Andy Schleck and Evans was down to 57 seconds and they both knew that the time trial would more than reverse their positions. Evans had also distanced Contador and Sanchez, proving his superiority in every discipline. He won the Tour with a 1-34 advantage over Andy Schleck.

FROM FALLER TO CHAMPION

Bradley Wiggins's 2011 Tour ended on a road in northern France, the pre-race favourite dumped out with a broken collarbone in one of the nervous crashes that litter the modern race's first week. Twelve months later, he went from faller to hero as Britain's first Tour de France champion. It was a consummate display from Wiggins, who was never out of the top two places overall, and his versatile Sky team.

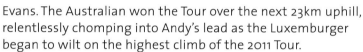

OPPOSITE: Bradley Wiggins is protected by his diligent Sky team-mates during the 2012 Tour.

TOP LEFT: Mark Cavendish continued to dominate Tour field sprints.

ABOVE: Cadel Evans leads Thomas Voeckler in the Alps during the 2011 Tour.

In the race's first mountain stage to La Planche des Belles Filles, compatriot and team-mate Chris Froome won while Wiggins donned a yellow jersey he would keep to the finish. Froome was Wiggins's only equal in the mountains, as defending champion Evans dropped away and the attacks of third-place finisher Vincenzo Nibali and Jurgen Vandenbroeck were kept at bay with steady, fast riding.

Team Sky's scientific, thorough approach helped to set them apart from the rest. Wiggins extended his advantage by winning the race's two long time trials and Froome finished second, 3-21 behind.

BELOW: Thomas Voeckler had France dreaming about a first home win since 1985, but he lost the yellow jersey and finished fourth overall in 2011.

A Race for the Ages

The 2011 Tour had it all: crashes, homegrown heroes, great racing, and a nailbiting finish. Add to that the first green jersey for Tour supersprinter Mark Cavendish and a record first Aussie Tour win for Cadel Evans and the 98th Tour will go down as a classic. The race route was not spectacular and that in itself was a spur for good racing as the favourites realised that the terrain itself was unlikely to force a final selection. They would have to attack, and as a result the racing was spectacular in the first week and in the Alps. When one of the stars attacked in the mountains the gaps opened slowly and there was no telling how the move would progress. That was in contrast to more recent times when one supercharged acceleration was often enough to decide the stage. Cycling's battle with doping had taken the sport to the brink but if cleaner cycling created a race like the 2011 Tour, it was worth every suspension and negative headline.

The 100th Edition of the Tour (2013)

The 100th edition had a spectacular route like no other, visiting the legendary places that made the Tour de France what it is today.

MODERN TIMES

The Tour de France is the high point of every cycling season, but given the historical significance of the 2013 race, it was set to capture the whole world's attention as never before. It was designed as a celebration of the preceding 99 editions, lauding the great champions and passing over the same roads where the Tour's greatest stories went down into folklore.

Modern Tour routes often have one or two "marquee" stages, including climbs of great difficulty or historical resonance to capture the attention of the public, but the 100th race was a feast, including all of the race's most iconic mountains, and a pilgrimage to the places that have helped make the Tour

de France legendary. L'Alpe d'Huez (twice) and the Col de la Madeleine were on the menu when the race reached the Alps.

It was a Tour for the climbers, with no fewer than four of the six mountain stages concluding with summit finishes. In addition, six mainland cities hosted either a stage start or finish for the first time, and, finally, the Tour remained within French borders for the first time in ten years.

While respecting history, the 100th Tour had a contemporary twist too, knitting exciting innovations into the fabric. That began with the unorthodox Grand Départ and three road stages on the Mediterranean island of Corsica, the only *région* of metropolitan France not previously visited by the race. German sprint giant Marcel Kittel won the first stage but it was the image of a team bus wedged underneath the finishing gantry that made the headlines.

The race then transferred to the Riviera for a team time trial around the city of Nice, won by Australian team Orica-GreenEdge, and headed west along the coast to Marseille, one of the six cities that hosted stage finishes in the original Tour de France.

In the Pyrenees there was a summit finish on Ax 3-Domaines where pre-race favourite Chris Froome won the stage and took the yellow jersey. The Tour continued to Bagnères-de-Bigorre, where Ireland's Dan Martin grabbed his first Tour stage win and, after a long transfer north, a showcase time trial finishing at Mont-Saint-Michel saw Froome finish second to popular German Tony Martin, extending his overall lead to three minutes.

After a long stage 15 finishing on the iconic Mont Ventoux, Froome confirmed his status as the complete Tourman, winning the stage after dropping Colombia's Nairo Quintana near the summit. A blockbuster finish was promised by back-to-back Alpine stages. One climbed L'Alpe d'Huez twice while the final mountain test concluded on the tough climb of Semnoz before a unique nocturnal finish on the Champs-Elysées in Paris.

"My dream is simple: that the kids of today and tomorrow dream of the Tour the way it made me dream 45 years ago."

CHRISTIAN PRUDHOMME

ABOVE LEFT: Corsica's magnificent coastline was the backdrop to a spectacular 100th edition Grand Départ.

LEFT: When a team bus got stuck on the finish line of stage one, organisers moved quickly to arrange an alternative finish. It was not needed as the bus was removed in time.

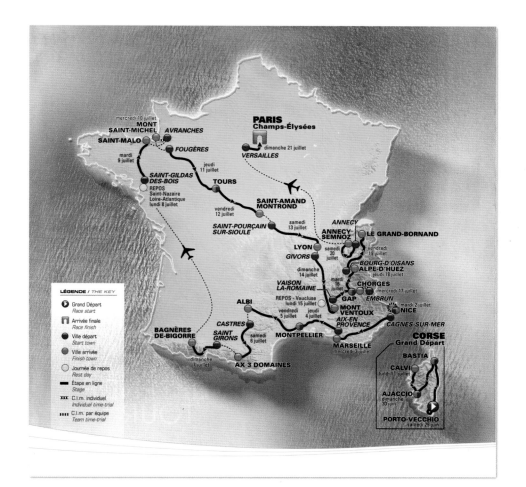

DATE	ÉTAPE	DÉPART	ARRIVÉE	KM
Samedi 29 juin	1re	Porto-Vecchio	Bastia	212
Dimanche 30 juin	2e	Bastia	Ajaccio	154
Lundi 1er juillet	3e	Ajaccio	Calvi	145
Mardi 2 juillet	4e	Nice	Nice (C.l.m. par équipe)	25
Mercredi 3 juillet	5e	Cagnes-sur-Mer	Marseille	219
Jeudi 4 juillet	6e	Aix-en-Provence	Montpellier	176
Vendredi 5 juillet	7e	Montpellier	Albi	205
Samedi 6 juillet	8e	Castres	Ax 3 Domaines	194
Dimanche 7 juillet	9e	Saint-Girons	Bagnères-de-Bigorre	165
Lundi 8 juillet	Repos	Saint-Nazaire - Loire-Atlantique		
Mardi 9 juillet	10e	Saint-Gildas-des-Bois	Saint-Malo	193
Mercredi 10 juillet	11e	Avranches	Mont-Saint-Michel (C.l.m. individuel)	33
Jeudi 11 juillet	12e	Fougères	Tours	218
Vendredi 12 juillet	13e	Tours	Saint-Amand-Montrond	173
Samedi 13 juillet	14e	Saint-Pourçain-sur-Sioule	Lyon	191
Dimanche 14 juillet	15e	Givors	Mont Ventoux	242
Lundi 15 juillet	Repos	Vaucluse		
Mardi 16 juillet	16e	Vaison-la-Romaine	Gap	168
Mercredi 17 juillet	17e	Embrun	Chorges (C.l.m. individuel)	32
Jeudi 18 juillet	18e	Gap	Alpe-d'Huez	168
Vendredi 19 juillet	19e	Bourg-d'Oisans	Le Grand-Bornand	204
Samedi 20 juillet	20e	Annecy	Annecy - Semnoz	125
Dimanche 21 juillet	21e	Versailles	Paris Champs-Élysées	118

TOTAL AVANT HOMOLOGATION 3 360 km

ABOVE: The official route and stage details for the 100th edition of the Tour de France.

With a win on the stage 17 time trial behind him, Froome and his Team Sky team-mates never looked in trouble despite a strong stage 20 win at Semnoz by Quintana which elevated the Colombian to second overall.

INTO THE FUTURE

Society and technology are moving on apace into the twenty-first century and the Tour de France has evolved too. As the world becomes more accessible with faster and more plentiful international transport links, we can expect more riders from all over the world to illuminate the race. Colombians made an impact on their first Tour in 1983, though the event had to wait more than a century for the first Australian and British winners. In more recent times, riders and teams from Africa, Israel and the Gulf states have broadened the Tour's global reach even further.

With Corsica seeing the Tour for the first time in the 100th edition, at last every corner of metropolitan France has seen the great race pass. France and its environs will never tire of

LEFT: Race leader Chris Froome passes Mont St Michel during the stage 11 time trial.

BELOW: Christophe Riblon heads to victory surrounded by thousands of Dutch fans on L'Alpe d'Huez during stage 18.

Christian Prudhomme

Christian Prudhomme is the seventh man to direct the Tour de France and the man principally responsible for the route of the 100th Tour. A tall, cheerful man from Normandy, Prudhomme developed a burning passion for cycling during afternoons spent listening to European races on the radio. Like his predecessor Jean-Marie Leblanc, he was a journalist, commentating on the Tour de France on French national television, before taking over his current position in 2006.

As the Tour expands, the director's role has become a bigger juggling act of jurisdiction. As well as organising the route of future courses, Prudhomme must talk to politicians and tourism boards and pull together race sponsors and logistics. It is also his duty to take responsibility when bad news sweeps in, and during his tenure as the Tour's helmsman Prudhomme has taken a hard-line stance against doping cheats.

the Tour, but there is a possibility of more ambitious Grands Départs on foreign soil – the oil-rich Arabian country of Qatar has already shown interest. Any start thousands of kilometres away from France will inevitably raise questions about such a departure from the race's deep roots. The future will be a battle to safeguard the Tour's traditional heart against ever-growing commercialism and different values – yet it can't be left behind either.

LOOKING GOOD AT 100

When it looked in the mirror, 100 editions young, the Tour de France could take some pride that in spite of scars and blemishes it was in good health. Through episodes of skulduggery that threatened the early races, two interruptions by World Wars, doping scandals and reshuffles in the organisation, it has not just kept going but grown into both a beloved French national and cultural institution, and a worldwide sporting behemoth.

Hundreds of thousands on each roadside stage and billions in front of televisions watched the peloton in their hi-tech kit as they rolled out of Porto-Vecchio at the start of the 100th Tour in 2013. How different it was from those 60 cyclists riding out on heavy bicycles from the outskirts of Paris in 1903. Different, yet essentially the same.

Youth follows the Brits (2012–2020)

Sir Bradley Wiggins became the first-ever British winner of the Tour de France in 2012. Chris Froome joined the greats with his fourth Tour win in 2017 and Geraint Thomas scored a first for Wales in 2018. The winds of change blew in at the end of the decade with Colombia and Slovenia producing young winners in Egan Bernal and Tadej Pogacar.

MODERN TIMES

100

Was there ever a better year for British cycling than 2012? In the perfect build-up to the Olympic Games in London, in July Bradley Wiggins began the celebrations early with a rock-solid victory in the 99th edition of the Tour. Wiggins's triumphant return to the London Games, winning the time trial gold medal, capped a summer of cycling success on road and track beyond the wildest dreams of GB cycling fans.

No one could have predicted that Sir Bradley's Tour win would be his last great hurrah on the road, and that he would not even have the opportunity to defend his Tour title in 2013. That was ostensibly due to his desire to target the Giro d'Italia in May which, had he won it, would have allowed him to ride the Tour as joint leader with Chris Froome on Team Sky.

Froome's strong riding in the mountains and time trials, plus a stage win and second place overall in the 2012 Tour, presented a dilemma that few teams ever have the luxury to face – how to compose a Tour de France team with the two outstanding favourites.

But Wiggins's abandon at the Giro and his frosty relationship with Froome made the decision to drop him from the 2013 Tour a tough but shrewd call by Team Sky principal Sir Dave Brailsford. And Brailsford was vindicated thanks to Froome's comprehensive victory in the 2013 Tour de France (see The 100th Edition of the Tour, pages 96–99). In just three years since its debut as an all-new outfit, Team Sky had produced the first British winner of the Tour. It had then clinically, some would say ruthlessly, moved on the following year, disposing of its most valuable asset, replacing him with a more youthful and ambitious Tour champion.

YORKSHIRE HOSTS 2014 START
Fittingly, the 2014 Tour de France Grand Départ featured three stages in England, with stages one and two in Yorkshire and the third stage heading into London to finish on The Mall outside Buckingham Palace. Climbs through the Yorkshire Dales and even Holme Moss failed to split the field but a steep uphill finishing climb in Sheffield was won by Italian hopeful Vincenzo Nibali,

TOP: Mark Cavendish is down, and out, of stage one of the 2014 Tour just metres from the finish line in Harrogate, Yorkshire.

ABOVE: Chris Froome wins stage 10 at La Pierre St Martin en route to his second Tour victory in 2015.

"My dream is simple: that the kids of today and tomorrow dream of the Tour."

CHRISTIAN PRUDHOMME

alerting defending champion Chris Froome that there is no such thing as an easy ride in the Tour.

Sprint champion Mark Cavendish needed no reminding how cruel the Tour could be. Winning stage one and wearing the yellow jersey in his home country had been a dream ever since the Yorkshire Grand Départ was announced. But in his eagerness to win the bunch finish in Harrogate he crashed heavily, injuring his shoulder. Cavendish's Tour was over before it had even started, gifting the limelight to German giant Marcel Kittel who took stages one and three, and two more after that.

There was more drama to come when the race returned to Europe, with Froome crashing and abandoning the race during the wet and hectic stage five which ravaged the field as it negotiated seven sections of cobbled lanes used in the notorious Paris–Roubaix classic. Man on form Nibali, already in the yellow jersey, delivered another blow to his rivals, finishing third on the stage and increasing his overall lead on the GC field to more than two minutes. When Alberto Contador also crashed out on stage ten, fracturing his leg, Nibali's command of the race was total and he won three mountain stages on the way to building a seven-minute lead in Paris.

FROOME RETURNS IN 2015

Four Grand Tour winners were among the 198 starters lined up for the opening prologue TT in Utrecht, Holland, for the start of the 102nd Tour de France in 2015. Former Tour winners Alberto Contador (2007, 2009) and Vincenzo Nibali (2014) were established champions and known quantities. The enigmatic Colombian Nairo Quintana came almost directly from his first Grand Tour win at the Giro d'Italia. African-born Brit Chris Froome, the 2013 Tour winner, had the might of Team Sky behind him but had yet to convince that he was robust enough to become a multiple Tour winner.

Dispelling all talk that he was a fragile crasher, Froome struck early and decisively in the crosswinds in Zeeland province on stage two, putting time into Quintana and Nibali. The following day, after an apocalyptic high-speed pile-up that resulted in the race being neutralised and yellow jersey-holder Fabian Cancellara's abandonment later that day, Froome finished a combative second on the vertiginous Mur de Huy, distancing all his GC rivals. This was the assertive, dominant and assured leadership that multiple Tour winners had shown flashes of in the past, and Froome was beginning to fit the mould.

On stage ten, the first mountain summit finish of the race at Pierre-Saint-Martin in the Pyrenees, Froome attacked with teammate Richie Porte, won the stage and put a minute into Quintana. American hope Tejay van Garderen lay in second place overall but quit the race in the final week through illness while lying in third. Only Quintana, who appeared to gain in strength while Froome faltered in the final week, made inroads into Froome's lead, pulling to within 22 seconds overall after gaining time on stages 19 and 20. It was a close finish, but in reality Froome was a convincing winner of his second Tour de France when the race paraded the Champs-Elysées the day after its alpine finale on L'Alpe d'Huez.

HISTORIC TRIPLE IN 2016

Chris Froome joined a select group of seven riders with three or more Tour wins and the manner in which he won the 103rd edition suggested that he was more than capable of adding to that tally. In this epic Tour, Mark Cavendish, after a fallow period during which Marcel Kittel and Andre Greipel had dominated Tour field sprints, made a sensational return to form with four stage wins. That took his total to 30, moving him above Bernard Hinault (with 28) into second place (behind Eddy Merckx with 34) in the all-time Tour stage winners list.

Once again the main challenges to Froome's reign came from Nairo Quintana and Alberto Contador, but the latter crashed heavily on a corner during stage one in Normandy. Contador soldiered on, but eventually abandoned the race on stage nine. Quintana had a relatively quiet Tour, failing to land any significant blows on Froome in the third week and finishing third overall, more than four minutes down. It fell to Frenchman Romain Bardet to excite the home fans with a skilful descent in the wet to win stage 19 while behind Froome slid out on a bend. He limited his losses by chasing back on team-mate Geraint Thomas's bike.

Froome took the yellow jersey after stage eight and held it all the way to Paris to record his most composed win to date. What the battle for the yellow jersey may have lacked in suspense, Froome more than made up for with moments of great panache, which included his kamikaze downhill attack on the Col de Peyresourde to win stage eight and his high-speed breakaway with Peter Sagan on stage 11. That was followed on the next stage when he was involved in a pile-up behind the TV motorbike on Mont Ventoux. Froome's bike was damaged in the crash, resulting in the extraordinary image of the yellow jersey-holder running with his broken bike in the final kilometre of the stage. In a controversial decision, the Tour gave Froome the same time as Bauke Mollema who was also involved in the incident but was able to continue on his bike.

In 2017, three-time winner Froome started as favourite at the Grand Départ in Dusseldorf, but he came to the 104th edition without a win in the preceding months and faced a course with some brutal hills and less time trialling kilometres than usual. Nevertheless, Froome impressed with a confident sixth place in the rain-hit opening time trial, which set him up for the yellow jersey after the first summit finish on stage five to La Planche des Belles Filles.

Italian Fabiu Aru wore yellow for two stages after winning on Peyragudes, but Froome was back in the lead by stage 14 and, despite small time gaps at the top, controlled the race to Paris. The 2017 Tour may not have been as successful for British riders as the 2016 edition, but with Geraint Thomas's stage one win and yellow jersey until stage four, only two stages were not led by a Brit in yellow. Simon Yates also won the best young rider's white jersey, finishing seventh overall, and Team Sky dominated the team competition.

Team Sky were happy to maintain a low profile during the first week of the 2018 Tour which saw the 105th edition pick its way from the start in the Vendée region, around the Brittany coast and on to the infamous cobbles where hot and dusty conditions saw Belgian Greg Van Avermaet retain the yellow jersey he had won after the stage three team time trial.

On stage 11's summit finish at La Rosière, Froome's faithful lieutenant, Welshman Geraint Thomas, was an emphatic winner and new wearer of the yellow jersey. When he won again the next day on L'Alpe d'Huez, distancing Froome and the other race favourites, it became Thomas's Tour to lose. He did not disappoint, holding off the challenge from runner-up Tom

Dumoulin in the third week while Froome rode defensively in third. In Paris, Thomas was crowned the first Welsh winner of the Tour.

Team Sky became Team Ineos in 2019. The new headline sponsor, a British chemicals company, matched the team's record-breaking budget, allowing Sir Dave Brailsford to evolve but not radically change his phenomenal Tour-winning outfit. All talk before the 2019 race was of how Chris Froome and Geraint Thomas would handle joint leadership roles, but when Froome sustained multiple serious injuries in a crash at the Criterium du Dauphine in June, Thomas started the 106th Tour as team leader. In only his second Tour, 22-year-old Colombian Egan Bernal joined the squad for the Grand Départ in Brussels after a strong build-up, but pledged to support the Welshman in the mountains.

In one of the most exciting and unpredictable Tours for decades, French double-stage winner Julian Alaphilippe took an early lead, but when the race entered the Alps for three brutal climbing stages into the final weekend, he was unable to respond to attacks from Thomas and, more damagingly, Bernal.

When stage 19 was dramatically cancelled due to a freak ice storm and mud slides on the road to Tignes, time gaps taken at the summit of the Col de l'Iseran elevated Bernal into the yellow jersey. He had been encouraged to attack by defending champion Thomas, and the Colombian was comfortably the best climber in the 2019 Tour. In Paris, Egan Bernal was hailed by thousands of his countrymen as the first ever Colombian winner of the Tour. With Thomas on the second step of the podium, the British team basked in the glory of seven Tour winners in eight years with four riders.

A superstar of the future, even younger than Egan Bernal, won the Covid-19 rescheduled (see boxout) 2020 Tour de France, confirming the decline of the old guard and ending the unprecedented winning run of the GB team Sky/Ineos Grenadiers. At 21, Tadej Pogacar was the youngest winner of the Tour since Henri Cornet (20) in 1904. The Slovenian produced one of the biggest upsets in Tour history on the penultimate stage, overhauling his compatriot in the yellow jersey, Primoz Roglic, in an epic time trial finishing on the Planche des Belles Filles climb. Australia's Richie Porte, after years of bad luck in the Tour, took a popular third place overall, while defending champion Bernal abandoned the race after stage 16 suffering from back problems.

2020 – the pandemic Tour

Not since 1946, the year after the Second World War, had the organisers contemplated a year without the Tour de France, but 2020 was a year like no other. As the global pandemic menaced continents, cycling events were cancelled or postponed. When ASO announced a new post-lockdown date at the end of August, many feared the race would be stopped somewhere between the Grand Départ in Nice and Paris. Roadside fans were urged to wear masks and banned from starts, finishes and climbs. Team bubbles ensured no rider tested positive for the virus, with only a handful of personnel quarantined. Despite the lack of fans, the riders served up a thrilling race right down to Irishman Sam Bennett's electrifying final stage-winning sprint on an eerily deserted Champs-Élysées.

ABOVE LEFT: In one of the Tour's greatest upsets, Tadej Pogacar toppled Primoz Roglic on the stage 20 time trial in the 2020 Tour.

OPPOSITE: Team Sky riders Geraint Thomas and Chris Froome share a moment in 2018.

Winners and Champions

From the super stylish bon viveur Jacques Anquetil to the voracious Eddy Merckx and the scientific dedication of Chris Froome, the race's great champions possess a range of different characteristics. But all of them showed the courage, tenacity and self-belief to win a host of Tours de France. Whether as the winner of the yellow, green, polka dot or white jerseys, to stand on the podium of the Tour de France in Paris is to reach the pinnacle of the sport.

LEFT: Triple Tour winner Chris Froome displays the tenacity and quick wit that it takes to be a Tour champion as he runs with his broken bike up Mont Ventoux on stage 12 of the 2016 edition.

100 Years of the Yellow Jersey

In 2019 the Tour celebrated 100 years of the introduction of the iconic yellow jersey, the unmissable symbol of the race leader. Starting in Brussels to honour 50 years since Eddy Merckx's first win, the 106th edition was a thrilling tribute to the Belgian great.

It's not difficult to understand how a rider becomes the leader of the Tour de France, but when the leader is tucked up in a speeding bunch it can be extraordinarily hard to actually spot him. This has been a problem for roadside fans over the years, craning their necks to catch a fleeting glimpse of the leading rider in the general classification. What better than a bright yellow top to ensure that a rider stands out from the pack? That was the thinking behind Tour founder Henri Desgrange's decision to have six jerseys knitted in the same colour as his sports newspaper *L'Auto* in 1919, at a stroke creating the most potent symbol of the Tour de France.

THE FIRST JERSEY
The first yellow jersey was just that, a jersey knitted from yellow wool that was given to French race leader Eugène Christophe in Grenoble during the rest day after the tenth stage. Christophe had been leading the race since the fourth stage and would wear the

"I didn't really believe I could win. I thought, 'That's for someone else, kids from Kilburn don't win the Tour.'"
BRADLEY WIGGINS

new yellow top for three days before losing it on the penultimate stage after breaking his forks in northern France. Christophe was the first wearer of the yellow jersey and the first rider to lose the lead through misfortune. He would not be the last, and stories surrounding the fortunes of wearers of the *maillot jaune* would become part of the folklore of the Tour in years to come.

FAMOUS FOR EVER
The yellow jersey doesn't bring bad luck, but when a rider in yellow suffers a crash or illness the story always makes the news,

RIGHT: Eugène Christophe (on bike) was the first man to wear the yellow jersey, but he finished third behind Firmin Lambot in the 1919 Tour de France.

FAR RIGHT ABOVE: Gastone Nencini won no stages when he led the overall classification on the 1960 Tour, but he was also third in the points classification and fourth in the King of the Mountains.

Eddy Merckx
Eddy Merckx holds the record for the number of days spent wearing the yellow jersey during the Tour de France. The Belgian five-time winner, nicknamed "The Cannibal", wore yellow on 96 occasions. Bernard Hinault is second with 75 days in the *maillot jaune*, while another five-times winner Miguel Indurain wore yellow 60 times. After Indurain comes fellow five-times winner Jacques Anquetil with 50 days and two-times champion Antonin Magne with 38.

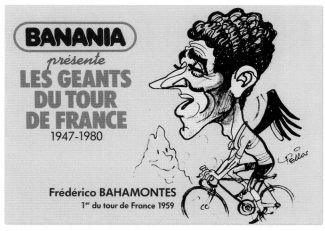

BANANIA présente LES GEANTS DU TOUR DE FRANCE 1947-1980

Frédérico BAHAMONTES
1er du tour de France 1959

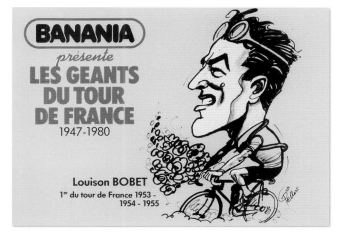

BANANIA présente LES GEANTS DU TOUR DE FRANCE 1947-1980

Louison BOBET
1er du tour de France 1953 - 1954 - 1955

BANANIA présente LES GEANTS DU TOUR DE FRANCE 1947-1980

Jacques ANQUETIL
1er du tour de France 1957 - 1961 - 1962 - 1963 - 1964

BANANIA présente LES GEANTS DU TOUR DE FRANCE 1947-1980

Gino BARTALI
1er du tour de France 1938 - 1948

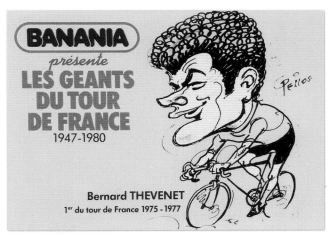

BANANIA présente LES GEANTS DU TOUR DE FRANCE 1947-1980

Bernard THEVENET
1er du tour de France 1975 - 1977

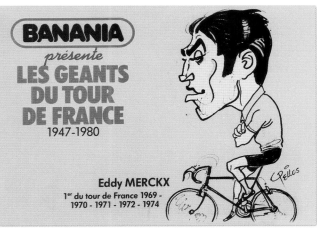

BANANIA présente LES GEANTS DU TOUR DE FRANCE 1947-1980

Eddy MERCKX
1er du tour de France 1969 - 1970 - 1971 - 1972 - 1974

RIGHT: Banania cards in the series "Giants of the Tour de France 1947–80". These eight giants, sketched by Pellos, wore the yellow jersey in Paris 19 times between them. Raymond [Poulidor] deserved one but …

OPPOSITE BOTTOM: Eddy Merckx, "The Cannibal," not only won more stages than any other rider, but also spent more days in yellow and, in the 1969 Tour, swept the yellow, green and polka-dot jerseys.

BANANIA présente LES GEANTS DU TOUR DE FRANCE 1947-1980

Raymond POULIDOR
3e du tour de France 1962
3e en 1963 - 2e en 1964 -
2e en 1965 - 3e en 1966 -
3e en 1972 - 2e en 1974 -
3e en 1976

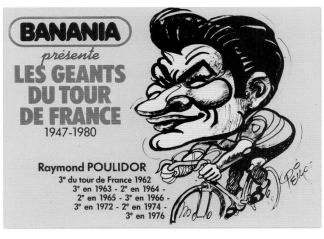

BANANIA présente LES GEANTS DU TOUR DE FRANCE 1947-1980

Luis OCANA
1er du tour de France 1973

even when that rider has no chance of taking the jersey to Paris. To wear the jersey is to achieve fame for at least a day, and to attract the attention of the world's media who like nothing better than to report on the noble suffering of a wounded and embattled race leader. In the 1983 Tour, the heroic suffering of the *maillot jaune*, Pascal Simon, showed the depth of reserves that a rider could draw on to hang on to the legendary jersey. Simon, a tall Frenchman riding for the Peugeot team, took the overall lead after distancing his rivals Laurent Fignon and Jean-René Bernadeau during a tough stage 10 across the Pyrenees to Luchon. Simon was a good climber and in the absence of Bernard Hinault that year, had a very real chance of continuing in yellow to Paris.

The next day a team-mate fell in front of him and Simon hit the road hard enough to fracture his left shoulder-blade. "I am prepared to suffer," he said. Bandaged, and gingerly helped into his yellow jersey each morning, Simon continued to lead the race over the next five stages, in agony every time he hit a bump in the road. A team-mate had to pick up his food bag, or *musette*, at the feed zones and another handed him a bottle to drink from. Finally, on stage 17 to L'Alpe d'Huez, Simon could ride no further and climbed into the ambulance, wiping the tears from his face with a sponge. The *maillot jaune* passed to the unfancied Fignon, who went on to win the 1983 Tour, a race that will always be remembered for Simon's brave heroics in yellow.

GREATNESS THRUST UPON THEM

Another trademark of the yellow jersey is its ability to inspire normal riders to feats of greatness. Countless riders since 1919 have begun the Tour as humble team workers, or with no particular ambition for a high overall placing, but have transformed themselves and sometimes their whole careers after getting a taste of the *maillot jaune*. Thomas Voeckler, for example, who led for ten stages of the 2004 Tour de France, was a French journeyman professional who had no designs on the overall standings but who took the lead after taking part in a long breakaway on the fifth stage from Amiens to Chartres (200.5km). Voeckler rode himself inside out to hang on to the lead through the Pyrenees, and by the time he lost it – and a lot more time – in the Alps to Lance Armstrong he was a French national hero. He would finish 18th overall, 31-12 behind Armstrong, but his fame in France was assured for the rest of his career.

In 2017 Geraint Thomas became the first Welshman to wear yellow and in 2018, after a stage win to La Rosière, he won the *maillot jaune* again, this time for keeps. He dominated the race from the Alps and Pyrenees all the way to Paris to become the first ever Welsh winner of the Tour de France.

One hundred years of the yellow jersey was celebrated in 2019, with fans and riders honouring the very first yellow jersey awarded to Eugène Christophe after stage 11 of the 1919 Tour de France. The 106th edition crackled with great racing and high drama from start to finish. With 16 different winners after the Grand Départ in Brussels and an absorbingly tight contest in the overall classification, French hopes soared when Julian Alaphilippe took the win and the yellow jersey after stage three, regaining it after stage seven and then sending home fans into raptures, winning the stage 13 time trial and heroically battling to hold onto yellow until stage 18.

ABOVE: First and second in the 1990 Tour Greg LeMond (left) and Claudio Chiappucci (right) share a bottle of water and a truce during the race.

RIGHT: As defending champion, Miguel Indurain wore the yellow jersey in the prologue of the 1993 Tour de France at Puy de Fou. After winning the prologue, he kept it for another two days.

Miguel Indurain

Miguel Indurain's Tour victories were achieved by crushing rivals in time trials and doggedly resisting them in the mountains. He won five consecutive Tours without claiming a point-to-point road stage, riding with great efficiency. Unlike more impetuous champions, such as Merckx or Hinault, his aim was not to lead the race for weeks on end.

Sir Bradley Wiggins

Sir Bradley Wiggins was Great Britain's first winner of the Tour de France in 2012. It was the culmination of an impressive metamorphosis, from heavier-set, multiple Olympic gold medallist on the track to mountain climber in just a few years. Born in the Belgian city of Ghent and brought up in the north London suburb of Kilburn, the tall and rake-thin Wiggins became popular for his iconic sideburns, rock'n'roll attitude and dry humour. His victory was built around wins in the race's two long time trials and strong, steady riding in the mountains. A passionate student of the sport, Wiggins achieved his win with engaging humility and sportsmanship. On the road to Foix, after several of his peers fell victim to punctures caused by carpet tacks strewn on the descent of the Mur de Péguère, he helped to slow down the race, earning the nickname "Le Gentleman" from the French press.

ABOVE: Bradley Wiggins is carried on the shoulders of his Sky team-mates as they celebrate his 2012 Tour win on the Champs-Elysées.

RIGHT: A yellow jersey from the 2004 Tour, signed by the ousted overall winner, Lance Armstrong.

BELOW RIGHT: Egan Bernal of Colombia, winner of the yellow jersey in its 100th year, stands atop the podium following his victory in the 2019 Tour.

By then, however, the sublime climbing power of a 22-year-old Colombian on the all-time great Tour team Ineos (formerly Team Sky), made the final result seem inevitable whenever the race climbed the legendary peaks in the Alps. Egan Bernal may have benefitted from the cancellation of stage 19, when an ice storm and mud slide blocked the road to Tignes, and a shortened stage 20 to Val Thorens, but with selfless backing from Tour defending champion Geraint Thomas, who finished second overall, the Colombian was hailed a worthy winner in Paris. Tour director Christian Prudhomme hailed it his "most beautiful Tour" and the contrast could not have been greater the following year, when the global pandemic cast a pall over a delayed 107th edition in September. In overall winner Tadej Pogacar, however, the yellow jersey graced the shoulders of the youngest champion since Henri Cornet in 1904.

MULTIPLE WINNERS OF THE TOUR DE FRANCE

Cyclist (country)	Wins	Years
Jacques Anquetil (France)	5	1957, 1961, 1962, 1963, 1964
Eddy Merckx (Belgium)	5	1969, 1970, 1971, 1972, 1974
Bernard Hinault (France)	5	1978, 1979, 1981, 1982, 1985
Miguel Indurain (Spain)	5	1991, 1992, 1993, 1994, 1995
Chris Froome (Great Britain)	4	2013, 2015, 2016, 2017
Philippe Thys (Belgium)	3	1913, 1914, 1920
Louison Bobet (France)	3	1953, 1954, 1955
Greg LeMond (USA)	3	1986, 1989, 1990
Lucien Petit-Breton (France)	2	1907, 1908
Firmin Lambot (Belgium)	2	1919, 1922
Ottavio Bottecchia (Italy)	2	1924, 1925
Nicolas Frantz (Luxembourg)	2	1927, 1928
André Leducq (France)	2	1930, 1932
Antonin Magne (France)	2	1931, 1934
Sylvère Maes (Belgium)	2	1936, 1939
Gino Bartali (Italy)	2	1938, 1948
Fausto Coppi (Italy)	2	1949, 1952
Bernard Thévenet (France)	2	1975, 1977
Laurent Fignon (France)	2	1983, 1984
Alberto Contador (Spain)	2	2007, 2009

Notes:

Alberto Contador was stripped of a third Tour victory (in 2010) and the overall classification was passed to Andy Schleck.

Lance Armstrong was stripped of all seven Tour victories 1999–2005 inclusive, but they were not reassigned.

The King of the Mountains

There has always been a fascination with the climbing aces of the Tour de France. Slight of build, with a taste for heroics and high theatre, they are cycling's most enigmatic characters.

ABOVE: Despite his origins in mountain-less Flanders, Lucien Van Impe emerged as one of the great climbers in Tour history.

BELOW: Renowned mountain cyclist Charly Gaul of Luxembourg, pictured during stage 17 of the 1955 Tour.

It took the Tour until 1933 to introduce a category and prize that recognised the talent of riders who specialised in cresting hills ahead of the rest. Big climbs had been a part of the Tour since 1905 when the race crossed the Ballon d'Alsace for the first time, after which it took in the Chartreuse mountains in 1907, followed by the Pyrenees in 1910 and the high Alps in 1911. During this period and into the 1920s winners tended also to be the best

climbers in the race, as mountain stages were so punishing that they were inevitably where the race was decided, given yawning time gaps and frequent dramatic mishaps. By the 1930s the Tour's national team format, improved equipment and the overall standard of riding encouraged a tactical approach that had more in common with Tours of the modern era than with the brutal elimination derbies of the early years.

Vicente Trueba of Spain, riding as an independent *touriste-routier*, was the first winner of the King of the Mountains in 1933. He didn't win a stage but was first over the Cols d'Aspin, Aubisque, Peyresourde, Tourmalet, the Vars, Ballon d'Alsace and the mighty Col du Galibier, and the "Spanish Flea" might well have done better than finish sixth overall had he been less of a nervous descender. He did not wear the dazzling white and red spotted top either, as the introduction of the polka dot jersey came many years later in 1975. It was sponsored by Poulain, the chocolate manufacturer, which had a product in similar polka-dot packaging.

DIFFERENT CATEGORIES

In the modern Tour de France there are five categories of climbs, with a "Four" allocated to rolling hills and a "One" awarded to serious mountain passes in the Alps and Pyrenees. The fifth category is confusingly named "*hors catégorie*", or without category, and is given to the few legendary Alpine and Pyrenean

"A true climber is a special thing, and training such a rider is more of an art than a science."
LUCIEN VAN IMPE

Charly Gaul

Charly Gaul won the Tour a year before his great Spanish rival Bahamontes. "The Angel of the Mountains" was a small man with thinning hair from Luxembourg, who excelled in bad weather. Unusually for a great climber, Gaul could also time trial, and in 1958 he beat Bahamontes against the watch up Mont Ventoux and then gained over 14 minutes on race favourite Raphaël Géminiani after an epic escape across the Chartreuse mountains in torrential rain. Unpredictable and secretive, Gaul won the mountains prize only twice, in 1955 and 1956, and became a recluse in retirement, putting on weight, growing a beard and living in a hut in the Ardennes.

ABOVE: Federico Bahamontes of Spain was a six-time winner of the King of the Mountains competition and is seen here soaring across the Alps to Briançon during the 1962 Tour.

RIGHT: King of the Mountains leader Lucien Van Impe ekes out a gap on rival Bernard Thévenet on the stage between Aurillac and Puy de Dôme in the 1975 Tour.

giants that play such a large part in the folklore of the Tour de France. Points are awarded at the summit of each climb on a sliding scale, weighted to favour the *hors catégorie* climbs above all others. A canny rider who may not be the best climber in the race can accumulate a sizeable cache of points on the smaller hills that pepper the first week of the Tour, and then afford to concede bigger scores in the Alps and Pyrenees when the battle for overall lead and individual stage wins hots up. This strategy paid off handsomely for Richard Virenque, the French heart-throb, who rode himself into the record books with seven wins in the *grand prix du montagne* classification between 1994 and 2004. Virenque was an able climber and a popular if controversial character, owing to his involvement in the Festina doping scandal of 1998. He could always guarantee vociferous support from his home nation during some particularly lean years for French riders.

Virenque holds the outright record for polka dot wins, a record that was previously shared between two of the all-time great

purist climbers of the Tour: Federico Bahamontes and Lucien Van Impe. To many, the Spaniard Bahamontes was the ultimate pure climber. He was a slight man with Brillo Pad hair and the face of an eagle. With knotted legs the colour of mahogany, he won the mountains prize in his first Tour appearance in 1954, gaining so much time on the bunch on the Romeyer climb that he is said to have stopped to eat an ice-cream at the summit while waiting for them to catch up. He later claimed that he had stopped because of a mechanical problem, but colourful anecdotes about "the Eagle of Toledo" suited him well. Impulsive and eccentric, Bahamontes lived for the mountains and had few ambitions for the overall classification until 1959, when a French team riven by dissent effectively handed the win to Bahamontes after he had won the stage 15 mountain time trial on the Puy de Dôme. Bahamontes was second overall in 1963 and won a record sixth mountains title in 1964, finishing third overall. He retired after abandoning the Tour a year later.

FLOURISHER FROM FLANDERS

Lucien van Impe won his six polka dot jerseys between 1971 and 1983, winning the Tour once in 1976 and making full use of his compact physique and toughening ascents of the short cobbled climbs of his native Flanders. In the modern era it has became much harder for pure climbers to win the Tour, thanks to the versatility of the overall contenders over the big mountains and in the time trials, which rarely favour the lightweight climbing aces. After Van Impe came Marco Pantani, whose electrifying attack to Les Deux Alpes in the 1998 Tour toppled Jan Ullrich and gave the maverick Italian enough of a margin to hold off the German in the final week. In recent years two Spanish climbers, Alberto Contador in 2007 and 2009 and Carlos Sastre in 2008, have won the Tour with great performances in the mountains and much improved rides against the clock.

In 2013 the diminutive Colombian Nairo Quintana became the latest pure climber with the talent to win a Grand Tour. In his debut Tour de France, aged 23, Quintana won the best climber's jersey, the young rider's classification and finished second overall to Chris Froome. With second place to Froome on Mont Ventoux on stage 15 and first on the final hilly stage 20 to Semnoz, Quintana just needed to improve his time trialling to win a Grand Tour. That he duly did to score a historic win in the Giro d'Italia in 2014. But overall victory at the Tour, and more specifically against Froome has eluded him so far. He finished second in 2015 and third overall in 2016.

Tours in the modern era have fewer time trialling kilometres and are designed to favour the strongest all-rounders, especially in the mountains. Only a great climber can win the modern Tour and that has taken some of the kudos from the polka dot jersey.

In 2018 Julian Alaphilippe was a worthy winner of the polka dot jersey after two mountain stage wins at Le Grand Bornand and Bagnères-de-Luchon. After Warren Barguil's double stage win and mountains title the year before, Alaphilippe became the second consecutive Frenchman to win the polka dot jersey in swashbuckling style. In the absence of an overall winner, French fans celebrated Alaphilippe's success with every

ABOVE: Eros Poli went down in Tour mountains folklore after his stage-winning solo breakaway up and over Mont Ventoux into Carpentras in 1994.

RIGHT: Thomas Voeckler accelerates to snatch King of the Mountains points from rival Frederik Kessiakoff on the way to Peyragudes in the 2012 Tour.

OPPOSITE LEFT: Tadej Pogacar won the mountains competition as well as the overall prize in the 2020 Tour.

Thomas Voeckler

Already the darling of the French public for his attention-grabbing spells in the yellow jersey in 2004 and 2011, Thomas Voeckler was a popular King of the Mountains in 2012. Having reinvented himself as an adept climber, he held off Swedish rival Frederik Kessiakoff. He secured the polka dot jersey by leading over the feared Pyrenean climbs of the Tourmalet, Aspin and Peyresoude on the way to victory in Bagnères-de-Luchon, his fourth stage win in the Tour de France. Cherub-faced Voeckler grew up on the Caribbean island of Martinique after his family moved there in his childhood to indulge his father's passion for sailing. Though some peers saw him as a show-off, Voeckler was a showman to fans, racing with attacking instinct, intelligence and individuality, gurning and chastising himself as he went up climbs.

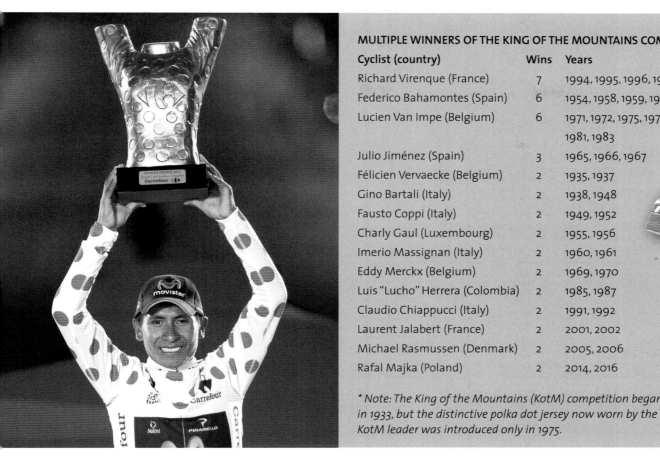

MULTIPLE WINNERS OF THE KING OF THE MOUNTAINS COMPETITION*

Cyclist (country)	Wins	Years
Richard Virenque (France)	7	1994, 1995, 1996, 1997, 1999, 2003, 2004
Federico Bahamontes (Spain)	6	1954, 1958, 1959, 1962, 1963, 1964
Lucien Van Impe (Belgium)	6	1971, 1972, 1975, 1977, 1981, 1983
Julio Jiménez (Spain)	3	1965, 1966, 1967
Félicien Vervaecke (Belgium)	2	1935, 1937
Gino Bartali (Italy)	2	1938, 1948
Fausto Coppi (Italy)	2	1949, 1952
Charly Gaul (Luxembourg)	2	1955, 1956
Imerio Massignan (Italy)	2	1960, 1961
Eddy Merckx (Belgium)	2	1969, 1970
Luis "Lucho" Herrera (Colombia)	2	1985, 1987
Claudio Chiappucci (Italy)	2	1991, 1992
Laurent Jalabert (France)	2	2001, 2002
Michael Rasmussen (Denmark)	2	2005, 2006
Rafal Majka (Poland)	2	2014, 2016

* Note: The King of the Mountains (KotM) competition began in 1933, but the distinctive polka dot jersey now worn by the KotM leader was introduced only in 1975.

"I race with one motto: win or bust!"

THOMAS VOECKLER

expectation that the 26-year-old from the Cher region had many years ahead of him to win stages and collect mountains jerseys. Riding for a Belgian team, Alaphilippe is one of the most exciting one-day racers in the sport today, and has a strong team behind him. He can climb, is not afraid to attack, and if his time trialling improves then his future as one of France's leading Tour riders is assured.

ABOVE LEFT: Nairo Quintana won the polka dot jersey in his debut Tour in 2013.

ABOVE RIGHT: A modern polka dot jersey, signed by Richard Virenque and with his sponsors added.

BELOW: Julian Alaphilippe pictured in the polka dot jersey at the 2018 Tour de France.

113

THE KING OF THE MOUNTAINS

The Story of the Green Jersey

To win the green jersey in the Tour de France you not only have to risk your neck in frequent bunch sprints, you must also survive three gruelling weeks across every terrain.

114

The green points jersey is awarded to the rider who accumulates the most points at stage finishes and during intermediate sprint "primes" along the route. It is considered second only to the yellow jersey in prestige, principally because it involves a full three-week campaign, unlike the more romantic competition for the mountains prize. The green jersey is worn by the best all-round sprinter, and points are weighted to favour the most consistently high-placed finisher on the flat stages, reduced for mountain stages and time trials. This also ensures that even the most dominating overall contender is unlikely to win both the yellow and green jerseys, as competing in the mass field sprints at the end of stages is not worth the risk. It is a mistake to assume that the best sprinter in the Tour will always win the green jersey, however, as there is a lot more to this prize than the ability to explode at 70kmh from a writhing mass of riders at the end of an arrow-straight boulevard. To wear green the rider must also survive the mountain stages when elimination for arriving outside the time limit is a very real possibility, as well as have enough in the tank to contest the flatter stages at the end of the third week.

LEFT: Wearing bib number 64, André Darrigade, a member of the France team, claimed this green jersey in 1959. The winner of 22 stages in his career, he also won the green jersey in 1961.

BOTTOM LEFT: André Darrigade of France wins a typical field sprint in St Gaudens during the 1959 Tour.

BELOW: Before Zabel, Sean Kelly was the ultimate green jersey. The versatile Irishman won four titles and finished fourth overall in the 1985 Tour.

Djamolidine Abdoujaparov

Djamolidine Abdoujaparov (left), who won the green jersey three times in 1991, 1993 and 1994, was one of the most spectacular and fearless sprinters that the Tour has ever seen. Muscular and compact, the Uzbek had the classic build of a sprinter but his method paid no more than lip service to the admittedly rough-hewn etiquette of sprinting. Head down, weaving all over the place and putting the machine under intolerable loads, "the Tashkent Terror" was a tangle waiting to happen. Within sight of the finishing line on the final stage of the 1991 Tour "Abdu" ploughed headlong in to a giant inflatable Coke can just metres from the line on the Champs-Elysées. He had won the green jersey already, but Abdoujaparov still had to finish the Tour, and it took him another 15 minutes to walk across the line, bloodied and tattered, helped by medics.

LEFT: Sprinter Djamolidine Abdoujaparov's unorthodox style bordered on reckless, but was thrilling to watch.

BELOW: Three-times green jersey winner Freddy Maertens takes the prestigious stage into Nice during the 1981 Tour.

BOTTOM: King of the Green – Erik Zabel holds the record for the most points wins at the Tour with six green jerseys.

"I haven't ridden with anyone who has that aura of strength. Iron man isn't enough, he's made of stainless steel."

ROBERT MILLAR ON SEAN KELLY

A run through the list of winners since the first green jersey was pulled on to the shoulders of Swiss Fritz Schaer in 1953 confirms that the prize has traditionally been won by the best roadman sprinters, but not always the fastest pure finishers from each era.

In recent times that has certainly been the case, the most notorious example being Mario Cipollini, without question the king of sprinting throughout the 1990s, who recorded 42 stage wins in the Tour of Italy – which remains the record – and who also achieved success at the Tour de France with 12 stage wins. In total the flamboyant Italian won 140 stages in various multi-stage events during his 16-year career. "Super Mario" had the best-drilled team, he had the lightning top speed and the élan, but he never won the green jersey – he just could not get over the Pyrenees or the Alps and, in what became an annual joke, would slip quietly away from the Tour after a week or so to perfect his tan on an Italian beach. Cipollini rode the Tour six times, but never made it to the Champs-Elysées.

RECORD HOLDER

Erik Zabel on the other hand was the type of rider who was made for the green jersey, and he set a new record by winning six times in an unbroken run from 1996 to 2001. The former East German might not have had the ballistic sprinting power of a rider like Cipollini, but in every other respect he was a more complete rider who could win classic one-day races and six-day events on the track. Zabel won 12 stages of the Tour but, more

"He's the fastest ever."

EDDY MERCKX ON MARK CAVENDISH

importantly, he had the ability to survive the high mountains and contest sprints when his team were either too tired to help him or were otherwise engaged protecting his long-time team-mate and overall contender Jan Ullrich.

Zabel's record number of points wins eclipsed that of the great Irish champion Sean Kelly, who held the previous best with four green jersey victories between 1982 and 1989. Kelly was in the same mould as Zabel, a phenomenal multi-talented rider with a pin-ball sprint and never-say-die attitude in the mountains. Kelly was the better all-rounder, taking fourth overall in the 1985 Tour, when he also won his third points jersey.

PHENOMENAL SAGAN

In his first Tour de France in 2012, Peter Sagan won three stages and his first green points jersey. The 22-year-old Slovakian could sprint with the best in the world but he was far from a "sit-in sprinter" and rapidly gained fans worldwide with his exuberant style of racing. In the mountains he was as powerless as other green jerseys of the past, and has never shown any interest in the final overall classification. But, away from the Alps and Pyrenees, Sagan is the most complete and exciting rouleur of modern times.

Sagan's record-equalling seven green jerseys between 2012 and 2019 have surpassed the previous all-time points jersey champion, Erik Zabel, but at 29 the Slovak could quite conceivably double that number considering his mastery in the competition. In his eight Tour de Frances so far, Sagan has won 12 stages and worn the yellow jersey on numerous occasions, albeit only in the first week of the race when there are multiple flat stages and sprint finishes.

Mark Cavendish

Mark Cavendish is the fastest sprinter of the modern era, and perhaps the best that the Tour de France has ever witnessed. He won 30 stages between 2008 and 2016, a prolific hit rate bettered only by Eddy Merckx. His deceptive, small build conceals an engine capable of searing, sudden acceleration. Cavendish has the mind of a champion too, possessing a burning competitive instinct and great self-assurance. His distinctive lead-out train of helpers was a familiar sight on flat stages of the late Noughties, stretching the bunch into a long strand before the "Manx Missile" finished the job off. Despite this, Cavendish had to wait until 2011 for his first green jersey. In preceding editions, he lost out to cannier, more consistent rivals Thor Hushovd and Alessandro Petacchi. Now, having won four times In a row at the Tour's finish on the Champs-Elysées, Cavendish is widely regarded as the all-time king of the sprinters.

ABOVE: Wannabe green jersey winners must suffer through the mountains. Green jersey Mark Cavendish digs deep on the road to Pinerolo in the 2012 Tour.

RIGHT: A green jersey from the 2004 Tour signed by Australia's Robbie McEwen.

MULTIPLE WINNERS OF THE GREEN JERSEY

Cyclist (country)	Wins	Years
Peter Sagan (Slovakia)	7	2012, 2013, 2014, 2015, 2016, 2018, 2019
Erik Zabel (Germany)	6	1996, 1997, 1998, 1999, 2000, 2001
Sean Kelly (Ireland)	4	1982, 1983, 1985, 1989
Jan Janssen (Netherlands)	3	1964, 1965, 1967
Eddy Merckx (Belgium)	3	1969, 1971, 1972
Freddy Maertens (Belgium)	3	1976, 1978, 1981
Djamolidine Abdoujaparov (UZB)	3	1991, 1993, 1994
Robbie McEwen (Australia)	3	2002, 2004, 2006
Constant "Stan" Ockers (Belgium)	2	1955, 1956
Jean Graczyk (France)	2	1958, 1960
André Darrigade (France)	2	1959, 1961
Laurent Jalabert (France)	2	1992, 1995
Thor Hushovd (Norway)	2	2005, 2009

ABOVE: Peter Sagan in green is a common sight in recent Tours, and the charismatic Slovakian has claimed an astonishing seven points classification victories.

RIGHT: Sam Bennett was the points winner in 2020, the first Irishman to win green since the great Sean Kelly in the 1980s.

In 2016, Sagan blitzed the Tour with three stage wins and a fifth green jersey. Expectations were high for a record-equalling sixth green jersey at the 2017 Tour de France but, following a crash with Cavendish on stage four, Sagan was controversially thrown out of the race by the UCI chief judge. The subsequent absence of both Cavendish, who fractured his shoulder, and Sagan may explain why Marcel Kittel won five stages, although in Paris the popular winner of the green jersey was the more versatile double stage winner Michael Matthews of Australia.

Sagan crashed again, during stage 17, in the third week of the 2018 Tour, but by then he had already won three stages and was safely in green. After a painful few days he rode into Paris to be crowned the sixth winner of the green points jersey. A single stage victory followed in 2019, but it was enough for Sagan to cruise comfortably to his record-breaking seventh points win.

The Story of the White Jersey

The white jersey is the young man's game, marking out the Tour's stars of tomorrow as prodigies upset the established order.

Run in conjunction with the general classification, the white jersey is awarded to the best-placed rider overall under 26 years of age on 1 January of the year preceding that Tour. In any year, roughly a fifth of the Tour de France's field meet that criterion. It is a chance for an ambitious young rider to stand out from the rest of the pack – which isn't too difficult in dazzling head-to-toe white.

A white jersey hopeful must be strong in the mountains to stand any chance of challenging. Winners are usually riders serving Tour apprenticeships at the beginning of their careers. Some have burst from anonymity to make this success an early milestone on the path to future Tour de France victory or stage wins; for others, the white jersey is the highlight of their careers.

The white jersey was introduced in 1975 and sponsored by Miko. For seven years previously, that colour had been worn by the leader of the combination classification. The young rider's classification was originally open to any rider who had been professional for less than three years; between 1983 and 1987, it was for Tour first-timers; and then it changed to the current format. A white jersey was not awarded to leading riders between 1989 and 1999, though the competition was still in place.

"I've realised one of my dreams, I took home a special jersey."

PIERRE ROLLAND

ON TO GREATER THINGS

Francesco Moser won the first white jersey in style, claiming the prologue and wearing the yellow jersey for six days on the way to finishing seventh in the 1975 edition. The rangy Italian went on to win many of the sport's biggest races, including the world championships and the cobbled Classic Paris–Roubaix three times, and to break the Hour record. It only takes a glance at the list of winners to recognise that the Italian was the first of several riders for whom a white jersey win was a harbinger of future stardom.

Winners of the white jersey rarely finish first in the Tour de France in the same year. In his very first Tour de France in 1982, bespectacled Laurent Fignon became the first man to do just that. Only Jan Ullrich, Alberto Contador and Andy Schleck have repeated the feat. American Greg LeMond was third in the 1984 Tour before going on to win his three Tours.

Fabio Parra, reared in the high mountains and rarefied air of Colombia, brought back a white jersey to South America in 1985

LEFT: Francesco Moser, the first winner of the white jersey, makes Felice Gimondi suffer in the 1975 Tour.

RIGHT: White jersey from the 2011 Tour, won by Pierre Rolland.

OPPOSITE: Australian Phil Anderson (middle) became the first non-European to win the white jersey in 1982.

with fifth place. He finished just 21 seconds ahead of Spaniard Eduardo Chozas to win the closest white jersey competition in Tour history. Three years later, he finished third overall, the only South American ever to finish on the Tour podium.

In 1994 the late Italian rider Marco Pantani burst on to the scene, winning his first of two consecutive white jerseys. He finished third overall, giving a glimpse of the natural ability in the mountains that would win him the yellow jersey in 1998.

MODERN PRODIGIES
Every now and then, a fresh-faced unknown reveals himself as a prodigy at the Tour de France and stomps over the established order. Jan Ullrich was one of the most precociously talented of them all. When he first emerged, combining time trial dominance with strength in the mountains, observers thought they were seeing the next Eddy Merckx. He holds the record for white jersey wins alongside Andy Schleck, taking the white jersey and finishing runner-up as a 22-year-

old in 1996, then winning it again in 1997 and 1998. Given the age restrictions, multiple wins of the white jersey are a rare achievement.

Alberto Contador followed his and Fignon's lead, winning the yellow and white jerseys in 2007. But in Paris that year, there was a strange twist. The white jersey was donned by Amets Txurruka, the man who finished third in the young rider's classification, a full 46 minutes behind Contador. Leaders in the Tour's classifications cannot wear two jerseys simultaneously: because Contador was clad in the yellow jersey and second-placed white jersey competitor Juan Mauricio Soler was also alongside him as King of the Mountains, Txurruka had the opportunity to take the spotlight.

TALENT SPOTTER
In 2011 French fans celebrated Pierre Rolland's successful run in the white jersey which included winning one of the race's key stages on L'Alpe d'Huez. Countryman Thibout Pinot did even

better in 2014, taking the white jersey and finishing third overall, confirming that while French cycling may not have a Tour winner, they are undoubtedly producing great young riders more than capable of standing on the podium in Paris.

Another youthful jersey record was set in 2013 when young Colombian star Nairo Quintana won both the climber's polka dot jersey and the young rider classification, as well as finishing second to Chris Froome in the General Classification. Quintana was also GC runner-up to Froome in 2015, when he took his second white jersey.

Quintana was just one of a clutch of promising young riders, many of whom have looked like future Tour winners, but who have yet to make the grade as contenders for the overall victory. They include 2012 white jersey winner Tejay van Garderen and 2016 best young rider Adam Yates. Adam's brother Simon took white in 2017, while young Frenchman Pierre Latour won white in 2018.

That all changed in 2019 and 2020, when both overall winners also won the young rider's classification. In 2019 Egan Bernal was just 22 years old when he took the yellow jersey with two

MULTIPLE WINNERS OF THE TOUR DE FRANCE WHITE JERSEY

Cyclist (country)	Wins	Years
Jan Ullrich (Germany)	3	1996, 1997, 1998
Andy Schleck (Luxembourg)	3	2008, 2009, 2010
Marco Pantani (Italy)	2	1994, 1995
Nairo Quintana (Colombia)	2	2013, 2015

Note: There has been an official competition for the best young rider at the Tour de France since 1975. Excluding the years 1989 to 1999, the leader of the young rider classification has worn a white jersey.

days to go and entered Paris as the first South American winner of the Tour. Bernal headed a super-talented influx of young riders who included Wout van Aert, Caleb Ewen and Enric Mas, all white jersey wearers from the 2019 race.

None, however, eclipsed the achievement of 21-year-old Tadej Pogacar at the post-lockdown Tour of 2020. The Slovenian became the youngest Tour winner since Henri Cornet in 1904, and one of eight champions who won the Tour on their debut. This hallowed company included Eddy Merckx, who Pogacar also matched as winner of three jerseys in Paris: the overall yellow; climbers' polka dot; and young rider's white.

Andy Schleck

Andy Schleck, who won the white jersey in 2008, 2009 and 2010, was a thoroughbred mountain climber. With a tall, angular body and the fresh face of a cub scout, his accelerations in the Alps and Pyrenees troubled rivals and made him a regular Tour challenger. Andy rode on the same team as older brother Frank, and the Luxembourg pair became well known for their teamwork. They finished second and third in the 2011 Tour. Schleck became better known for his second places in 2009 and 2011 rather than his white jersey-winning feats. For all his poise going up, his lackadaisical approach to descending and poor time trialling ability contributed to his near misses. Schleck never stood on the top step of the podium in Paris, but he was awarded victory in the 2010 Tour a year and a half later because of winner Alberto Contador's positive test for clenbuterol.

Other Tour de France Jerseys

Beyond the battles for the yellow, green and polka dot jerseys, the Tour has a host of no less keenly contested competitions.

122

The other jerseys and competitions in the Tour de France all offer prestige, prize money and publicity. For fans, it throws up interesting sub-plots to the main story. With so many things to race for, the humblest team or rider has something to pursue, whether it's the yellow jersey or the *lanterne rouge*.

First there is the team classification, a day-to-day and overall contest calculated by adding the times of the three best riders per team on classification every day. It was introduced when the Tour switched from manufacturer-based to national teams for the 1930 race. The leaders were historically denoted by the wearing of yellow caps. That changed to yellow numbers, and the 2012 Tour saw a new system of showing the leaders: yellow helmets. Winners Radioshack-Nissan chose not to wear them.

The competition is usually won by the team with the best strength in depth: T-Mobile won for three years in a row in 2004. Teams rarely approach the Tour with team classification victory in mind, but as the race progresses, it can become a comfortable fallback option, carrying decent prize money, if an individual leader has a poor race. It is also an opportunity for a whole team to mount the rostrum in Paris, an image

which can be manna from heaven for team sponsors hungry for publicity.

A PRIZE FOR THE FIGHTERS

The Tour is not all about winning. It has long respected valiant efforts to escape the peloton and panache. In 1952, the Prix de la Combativité was introduced. It is awarded to the rider with the most fighting spirit – showing bloody-minded persistence rather than pugilism, mind. At the end of every stage, a panel comprising members of the race organisation and media decides the winner. It is a competition for the plucky underdogs, normally awarded to a member of the day's breakaway. Rather than donning a jersey, the day's winner is denoted by a white race number on a red background.

At the end of the Tour, an overall prize is awarded for the whole race's most combative rider. Often bored with sitting in the bunch, Jacky Durand made it his mission to go up the road in brave, often doomed breakaways. His against-the-odds tactics won him a legion of fans – and several big races, including the 1992 edition of the Tour of Flanders. Durand was

"Sometimes 100 kilometres of riding alone in the Tour de France has more significance than a win in another race."

JACKY DURAND

BELOW: Tony Hoar (right), the 1955 Lanterne Rouge "winner", brings up the rear with Henri Sitek.

OPPOSITE: Swiss revelation Marc Hirschi was the outstanding winner of the most combative rider award in the 2020 Tour.

Lanterne Rouge

It is both a noble touch and a sign of the Tour's gruelling nature that the man who finishes last in every Tour is remembered along with the first. It is so-called because of the red lantern on the final wagon of old trains which let stationmasters know that a passing train's carriages were still attached. Belgian Wim Vansevenant has finished as *lanterne rouge* the most times, in 2006, 2007 and 2008. The last-placed man can enjoy a post-Tour boon in publicity and earnings, and some riders have made it their aim. Austrian Gerhard Schönbacher accomplished it in 1979. The Tour organisers grew tired of the attention this last-place fight received, and the following year they introduced a rule between stages 14 and 19 that meant the last-placed rider overall each day was excluded. No matter: Schönbacher made sure he stayed second-last each day and pedalled into Paris as *lanterne rouge* again.

124

recipient of the Prix de la Combativité in 1998 and 1999. Eddy Merckx has won it on four occasions, the most in history.

Standout performers in recent Tours include French climber Romain Bardet who took a stage win and raced aggressively throughout to win the combativity prize in the 2013 Tour de France. Bardet finished ninth overall to Chris Froome and a year later he put in a daring attack in the rain in the finale of stage 19 to take the stage and jump from fifth to

ABOVE: Bernard Hinault, in the gaudy combination classification leader's jersey, leads Greg LeMond on L'Alpe d'Huez in the 1986 Tour.

LEFT: Attack! Jacky Durand (right) does his best to stay away in another audacious breakaway on stage seven of the 1999 Tour.

OPPOSITE: The jersey winners of the 1988 Tour: Erik Breukink (white), Eddy Planckaert (green), Pedro Delgado (yellow), Steven Rooks (polka dot and combination) and Frans Maassen (intermediate sprints).

second overall. Winner of the 2016 combativity award was, not surprisingly, the irrepressible Peter Sagan who appeared in many breakaway moves en route to winning a fifth green jersey.

DISCARDED JERSEYS

Several jerseys have come and gone in the Tour de France. The most eye-catching was the combination jersey. Introduced in 1968, it was a strange points-based competition combining the yellow, green and King of the Mountains jerseys. It was calculated on a daily basis using the rider's ranks in those three classifications: the lower the score, the better. Eddy Merckx won five times, scoring a perfect three in 1969.

After twice being taken out and put back in for periods, the competition was discontinued in 1989, seen as an

anachronism. It was; no modern rider could hope to score well in three such disparate competitions. Mid-stage primes in the Tour now contribute to the points competition (green jersey), but between 1971 and 1989, points gained there contributed to another classification: the intermediate sprints competition. Sean Kelly was a three-times winner. The leader wore a red jersey, though this was introduced only in 1984.

There have been some weirder prizes over the years. Journalists on the race annually award a Prix Citron to the most unhelpful rider – an appropriate label for sour behaviour. Laurent Fignon and Lance Armstrong were both "winners" of this dubious accolade. There have also been prizes for the rider with the most bad luck. Fernand Picot won it in 1956 after finishing second in the points classification and on two stages; he never did win a Tour stage in his career.

Customs and Traditions

The Tour peloton is a community on two wheels, with many unwritten rules. For instance, it's bad form to challenge a rival who has suffered a mechanical mishap or is answering a call of nature. Superstition also retains a place in the modern Tour: some riders who are given the number 13 *dossard* (start number) elect to turn it upside down, to avoid bad luck.

LEFT: Fabian Cancellara honours Tour tradition by flipping his unlucky 13 while wearing the yellow jersey during the 2010 Tour de France.

Le Grand Départ

In the early years the Tour de France started and finished in Paris. Modern Tours rarely start in the capital and every few years the race begins in another country altogether.

In 2003 the Tour de France celebrated its centennial by visiting all six of the stage towns that featured in the 1903 Tour. The 90th edition of the race would, like all the others, finish in Paris, but this time around it would start there too, not outside a bar on the outskirts of town as it had done in 1903, but from under the unmistakable symbol of the Eiffel Tower right in the centre of town. After many years of Tour starts in French and European cities Le Grand Départ had come home for the first time since 1963.

Montgeron is a commune of south-east Paris, 18.5km from the centre. The Reveil-Matin bar is credited as the site of the first Grand Départ of the Tour, although roadworks caused the actual start to be moved to a tree-lined avenue nearby. It was at the Reveil-Matin that the 60 starters in the 1903 Tour signed on and, having paid their 10-franc entry fee, rolled down the road and were sent on their way with a pistol shot in the air by the official starter Georges Abran.

HOME IS WHERE THE HEART IS

Paris is the home of the Tour; it was where Tour founder Henri Desgrange lived and worked, and it was also the place where a big crowd was guaranteed in the early years of the Tour, before the race went to the provinces where the local response was harder to predict. Paris was where the offices of Desgrange's newspaper *L'Auto* were located, and in 1904 the courtyard of the office was used to inspect

ABOVE: In 1954 the Tour began in Amsterdam – the first Grand Départ outside France.

LEFT: The 1987 Tour began in Berlin, West Germany, less than two years before the Berlin Wall came down.

SPREADING THE WORD

The Grands Départs to have taken place outside mainland France:

1954	Amsterdam (Netherlands)
1958	Brussels (Belgium)
1965	Cologne (Germany)
1973	Scheveningen (Netherlands)
1975	Charleroi (Belgium)
1978	Leiden (Netherlands)
1980	Frankfurt (Germany)
1982	Basel (Switzerland)
1987	West Berlin (West Germany)
1989	Luxembourg City (Luxembourg)
1992	San Sebastian (Spain)
1996	s'Hertogenbosch (Netherlands)
1998	Dublin (Republic of Ireland)
2002	Luxembourg City (Luxembourg)
2004	Liège (Belgium)
2007	London (Great Britain)
2009	Monaco
2010	Rotterdam (Netherlands)
2012	Liège (Belgium)
2013	Corsica (France)
2014	Leeds (Great Britain)
2015	Utrecht (Netherlands)
2017	Düsseldorf (Germany)
2019	Brussels (Belgium)

Grand Frenzy

When the Tour comes to town the whole place goes Tour crazy. For the five days or so during which the race is arriving, setting up, conducting medical checks, presenting the riders and of course holding the opening prologue TT and the start of stage one, the town belongs to the Tour. Modern Tours, and Grand Départ towns, make the most of pre-Tour fever which builds on an hourly basis as the press and TV corps arrive in town and begin their three-week blizzard of stories and images. Everything is reported, from the riders getting their health checks, to mechanics assembling bikes and finally, on the night before the prologue, the glitzy presentation ceremony for all the teams. In 1990 the Tour gave the Futuroscope theme park in Poitou-Charentes a big publicity boost.

"While the Tour confirms its international vocation, London boosts its dynamic, sporting image."

JEAN-MARIE LEBLANC, TOUR DEPUTY DIRECTOR, SPEAKING OF THE 2007 TOUR

and stamp each competitor's bicycle before the race once again headed off in the direction of Lyons for stage one. That year the Tour came close to failure when it was plagued by cheating and terrorised by partisan supporters in the provinces. It survived, and from then on Desgrange played safe with the Départ, starting the race from Paris until 1925. Paris returned to favour a couple of years later and from 1927 to 1950 it again hosted the start of stage one. Then there was a long break, until the 50th Tour in 1963, followed by a longer one until the centenary was marked under the Eiffel Tower in 2003.

The first town outside Paris to host the Grand Départ was Evian, on the south bank of Lake Geneva in the Haute Savoie region of France, in 1926. But the organisers did the town no favours by flagging away the race at two o'clock in the morning on 20 June. This was the longest Tour de France in Tour history; it covered 5,745km, which might explain why the field were given an early start. Dull racing in the early stages persuaded Desgrange to return the start to Paris, which he did the following year and kept it there for another 23 years until 1950. During that time the Grand Départ began to realise its potential with appearances by stars of the stage such as Josephine Baker, who was invited to start the race from Vesinet, 18km west of Paris, in 1933. That

ABOVE: In 1990, the Tour's Grand Départ brought the Futuroscope film theme park in Vienne, near Poitiers, to the attention of the entire world.

year's race was sponsored by Fyffes bananas, bunches of which were employed to maintain Baker's modesty during her risqué stage act.

A move away from Paris for the Grand Départ was one of several changes to the route of the 1951 Tour. Under the post-war direction of Jacques Goddet, who took over from Desgrange after his death in 1940, the Tour became increasingly adventurous in its routing. Metz, in the north-east, hosted the first stage to Rheims and must have been deemed a success – there would be only two more official Paris starts thereafter. Civic prestige and the financial benefits of having the Tour de France in town were not lost on the many French Grand Départ towns that followed, and over the years the Tour has visited every corner of France.

CROSSING NEW BOUNDARIES

Neighbouring countries have also coaxed the Tour beyond its borders. In 1954 the Dutch capital Amsterdam became the first non-French city to hold the Grand Départ. Belgium followed in 1958, with Brussels, and then the German city of Cologne, in 1965, which saw the race pass through Belgium en route to Roubaix at the end of

day two. Dutch influence and enthusiasm resulted in a return trip to Scheveningen for the 1973 Départ, when a short prologue time trial, first introduced in 1967, gave the city two bites of the cherry with the prologue on Saturday and the start of stage one the next day. Holland scored again in 1978, when Leiden got in on the act.

German interest in the race was confirmed in 1980 with Frankfurt getting the Grand Départ nod, and Basel broke Switzerland's duck in 1982. In 1987 the Tour travelled further afield than ever before – to the still divided Berlin in West Germany, celebrating its 750th anniversary and that city's long association with track and road racing. Luxembourg city waved the Tour on its way in 1989, a race which ended with the closest winning margin in Tour history – just eight seconds separating Greg LeMond and Laurent Fignon.

ACROSS THE PYRENEES

Finally Spain got its Grand Départ in 1992, when San Sebastian honoured its Tour winner from the year before. Miguel Indurain did them proud, winning the prologue and his second of five consecutive Tours. The Dutch town of s'Hertogenbosch waved off

LEFT: Not a centimetre of roadway is visible as the riders negotiate the Passage du Gois at the start of the 2011 Tour.

BELOW: The bunch fans out across the line as it prepares to start in Luxembourg in the 1989 Tour.

OPPOSITE TOP LEFT: Dublin hosted the start of the 1998 Tour – the peloton streams out of the Irish capital at the start of stage one.

OPPOSITE TOP RIGHT: The clock starts ticking on Edvald Boasson Hagen's Tour de France as the Norwegian champion leaves the prologue start-house in Rotterdam in 2010.

OPPOSITE RIGHT: Masks and no crowds, the pandemic Tour of 2020 was like no other.

the 1996 Tour, and then in 1998 the race went even further afield than Berlin when the Grand Départ was staged in Dublin. Not far enough away, though, to escape the whiff of scandal that began to circulate as the Tour headed south through the Emerald Isle; it finally hit the headlines as the Festina case which laid bare the entrenched level of doping within the sport and which very nearly annulled that year's race. Since then the Tour returned to Luxembourg in 2002, was a big hit in London in 2007 and Rotterdam in 2010. In 2012 Liège in Belgium hosted the start of the 99th Tour, while the last *département* in France to see the Tour, Corsica, hosted Le Grand Départ in 2013.

In 2014 the Tour Grand Départ visited Great Britain for the fourth time, with the Yorkshire city of Leeds hosting the opening ceremony and first road stage from Leeds to Harrogate. Massive crowds confirmed cycling's post-Olympic popularity had not abated and after a second road stage from York to Sheffield, the race prolonged its British love affair with a third stage from Cambridge to London.

One year later the Tour returned to its more traditional fan base with a sixth visit to the Netherlands, this time Utrecht, where the field began the race with a 13.8km prologue time trial. Winner Rohan Dennis of Australia wore the yellow jersey for stage one from Utrecht to Zeeland, where strong crosswinds split the race, creating time gaps which would put eventual race winner Vincenzo Nibali in command before French soil was reached.

In 2016, the 103rd edition of the Tour commemorated D-Day and the Normandy landings with a Grand Départ opening stage from Mont-Saint-Michel to Utah Beach. This was the first time that the Tour had started in the Manche *région* of France. The opening ceremony was held in Saint-Mère-Église in tribute to the first allied soldiers landing in Normandy in 1941.

Germany was awarded hosting honours for the Tour Grand Départ for a fourth time in its history, this time in Düsseldorf in 2017. There was a 13km prologue and a road stage from the town, which left Germany the same day, the stage finishing in Liège, Belgium.

Returning to France for the 105th edition of the Tour in 2018, the Grand Départ took place in the Vendée region on the west coast. Belgium hosted the 2019 race start from Brussels, where the race

celebrated 50 years since the great Eddy Merckx won the first of his five Tour victories. Merckx was born on the outskirts of the Belgian capital and after being honoured at the Grand Départ, the first two stages remained in and around Brussels, with an opening road stage followed by a team time trial on stage two.

Corsica

The venue for the start of the 100th edition of the Tour de France was a grand departure from tradition. Corsica, the last *région* of France previously unvisited by the Tour, provided a sense of completion and fulfilled wanderlust. Transporting the Tour caravan across the sea was a logistical challenge, its compensation being the wild, stunning scenery on Corsica, nicknamed "the Island of Beauty". Corsica's government budgeted 2 million Euros to host the race for the opening three days. Given its mountainous terrain, the island delivered a Grand Départ like no other. It started with a 200km flat stage from Porto-Vecchio (won by Marcel Kittel) to Bastia, rather than a prologue time trial, before two hillier road stages. The island, which gave the world both Napoleon and vendetta, did not disappoint as the Grand Départ *par excellence* of the 100th Tour de France.

The Great Climbs

From the mysterious Pyrenees to the Technicolor Alps and all high-altitude points in between, the Tour is very much defined by its mountain stages.

Mont Ventoux is the most feared climb in the Tour de France. It is not in the Alps or the Pyrenees, nor is it the highest peak in the Tour – the Col de la Bonnette, first climbed in 1962, and only twice since then, takes that accolade at 2,802m. The Ventoux is a barren volcanic rock that stands sentinel in the Vaucluse. Its smooth, conical peak can be seen from miles around, with the summit observatory tower at 1,909m the only evidence of life. At the bottom of the climb there is some vegetation, but it cannot survive the scorching temperatures and scything mistral wind that creates a bleak landscape of scree further up the 21km climb. In 1967 the highest wind ever recorded on the summit was measured at 320kmh (199mph).

AN UNFORGIVING GIANT

Featuring in the Tour 16 times since it was first included on the route in 1951, the "Giant of Provence" gained a reputation as a climb that spread fear throughout the peloton. In 1955 French rider Jean Mallejac collapsed 10km from the summit and had to be revived by the race doctor. He survived, but was taken to hospital in a state of delirium. On the same day Swiss star Ferdi Kübler, winner of the Tour five years earlier, was also struck down by the pitiless sun and almost certainly the effects of amphetamines. He began weaving across the road and was then seen stumbling into a café. He reappeared, remounted his bike and set off in the opposite direction to the race. He was never the same rider again. Twelve years later British champion Tom Simpson also collapsed on the Ventoux, and there was nothing

"You are murderers, yes, murderers."
OCTAVE LAPIZE TO TOUR OFFICIALS, SUMMIT OF THE AUBISQUE, 1910

RIGHT: The distinctive leather helmet worn by Frenchman Jean Robic, one of the first riders to seek protection from perilous mountain passes.

BELOW LEFT: Octave Lapize is reduced to walking on the Col d'Aubisque in 1910, the year he denounced the Tour organisers as "murderers".

BELOW: A huge post-war crowd stands in awe of the great Fausto Coppi as the Italian heads for overall victory in his first attempt at the Tour in 1949

TOP: The long and winding road up L'Alpe d'Huez, with its famous 21 hairpins, makes for an impressive aerial view.

RIGHT: The bunch makes its way up the Col du Tourmalet in the 2010 Tour.

LEFT: Tom Simpson receives medical attention at the top of Mont Ventoux in the 1967 race.

Death on Ventoux

Tom Simpson's death on Mont Ventoux in 1967 robbed Britain of a great cyclist, and his memorial on the climb is a grim reminder of the dangers of cycling and doping. Simpson was Great Britain's first world road race champion in 1965 and was also a winner of one-day classics such as the Tour of Flanders, Milan–San Remo and the Tour of Lombardy. In 1962 he was the first Briton to wear the yellow jersey, finishing sixth overall in a result which he was convinced he could improve upon. In 1967 Simpson's Tour ended 3km from the summit of the Ventoux, where he collapsed while trying to stay with the leaders. Despite the efforts of the Tour doctor he was helicoptered off the mountain and pronounced dead at Avignon hospital. Cause of death was declared to be the effects of heat combined with amphetamines and alcohol.

the doctor could do to revive him. A memorial to Simpson stands a few hundred metres below the summit as a reminder to all bike riders of the very real dangers of this exposed and lifeless place. Simpson was the second rider to die while riding the Tour, the Spaniard Francisco Cepeda having been killed while descending the Galibier in 1935. The third Tour death also occurred in the mountains – Fabio Casartelli was mortally wounded on the descent of the Col de Portet d'Aspet in 1995.

After Mont Ventoux, L'Alpe d'Huez is a close second in the list of iconic Tour climbs. First crested on stage 10 in 1952 – the year that the Tour also included for the first time two other great climbs, the Puy de Dôme and Sestriere – the switchback ascent to the Alpine ski resort at 1,860m has become a Tour regular, celebrating its 29th visit in 2013. At 13.9km, with an average gradient of 7.9 per cent, it is not the hardest mountain to ride up on a bike, but thanks to some legendary battles over the years and its popularity with spectators, L'Alpe d'Huez has become Tour hallowed ground.

Col du Galibier

The Col du Galibier is not the steepest or longest mountain in the Alps, but it is one of the most respected, owing to its height and the fact that it has featured no fewer than 33 times in the Tour. On its first appearance in 1911, only three riders did not resort to walking. Marco Pantani orchestrated his 1998 Tour victory on the Galibier when he attacked Jan Ullrich in a freezing Alpine deluge, putting almost nine minutes into him by the finish on Les Deux-Alpes. It was not until 2011 that the climb staged a summit finish, the highest in race history at 2,645m, to celebrate the Tour's hundredth crossing of the Alps. Andy Schleck embarked on a 60km escape to victory, as he attempted to wrest the yellow jersey away from rival Cadel Evans. Desgrange, a man drawn to feats of derring do, would have liked that.

"All one can do before the Galibier is doff one's hat and bow."

HENRI DESGRANGE

ABOVE: Noël Amenc cuts a lonely figure on the Galibier during the 1921 Tour.

BELOW: La Planche des Belles Filles in the Vosges was the scene of one of the biggest upsets in Tour history at the 2020 Tour.

134

It was the first summit finish in the Tour, and first to the top was Italian "Campionissimo" Fausto Coppi who also took the yellow jersey, holding on to it from there to Paris. Its 21 hairpin bends are numbered from the bottom, with each plaque also recording the names of L'Alpe d'Huez winners down the years.

INTO THE PYRENEES

Wild, mysterious and often shrouded in mist, the Pyrenees were first visited by the Tour in 1910, and the mighty Col du Tourmalet was and still is a formidable obstacle. Before it was included in the 1910 race, Tour founder Henri Desgrange dispatched a trusted aide in his car to reconnoitre the climb, but far from the 2,115m summit he was stopped by heavy snow and had to go on foot to the top. From there he sent a telegraph to Desgrange – "perfectly

practicable" was his assessment. The Pyrenees have featured in most Tours since then, often before the Alps in post-war Tours, and are generally considered to be less damaging to the peloton. The highest Tour climb in the Pyrenees is the Port d'Envalira at 2,407m. Climbs such as the Portet d'Aspet, Peyresourde, Aspin and Aubisque that featured in the 1910 race are still used in modern Tours – as is the more recently included but equally imposing challenge of Luz Ardiden. They are just as popular as their Alpine counterparts with fans from France and more so Spain, into which the race has often extended via the Pyrenees.

The Ballon d'Alsace in north-east France was the first climb to be included in the Tour, in 1905, and the Pyrenees was the first great mountain range visited by the Tour (1910). The high Alps followed a year later, with the 2,556m Galibier climbed on stage five from

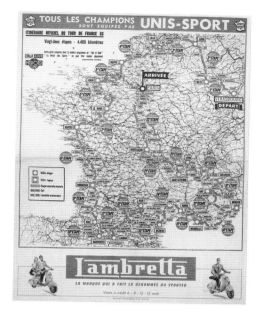

ABOVE: Small, but precious, this map plots the route the cyclists will take and also shows where Louison Bobet would win the Tour in 1953 – in the mountains.

BELOW RIGHT: Richie Porte crashed out on the scary descent of the Mont du Chat on stage nine of the 2017 Tour.

FAMOUS *HORS CATÉGORIE* CLIMBS

Mountain	Total climbs	Ht (m)	First HC	Most recent
Alpe d'Huez	30	1,860	1979	2018
Col du Tourmalet	58	2,115	1980	2018
Col du Galibier	34	2,645	1979	2019
Col de la Madeleine	26	1,993	1980	2020
Col d'Aubisque	47	1,709	1980	2012
Col de la Croix-de-Fer	20	2,067	1989	2018
Luz Ardiden	7	1,715	1985	2011
Col d'Izoard	26	2,360	1986	2019
Col de Joux-Plane	12	1,691	1981	2016
Plateau de Beille	6	1,780	1998	2015
Mont Ventoux	16	1,909	1987	2016
Pla d'Adet	9	1,669	1981	2005
La Plagne	4	1,980	1984	2002
Hautacam	5	1,560	1994	2014

Note: The organisers of the Tour de France established the Hors Catégorie *level of difficulty in 1979.*

Chamonix to Grenoble (366km), and from then on climbs such as the Col d'Allos, the Col d'Izoard, the Col de Glandon, the Col d'Iseran, the Col de Vars, Morzine, the Col de Madeleine, Courchevel and Les Deux Alpes have all played their part in Tour-winning exploits. A memorial monument to Tour founder Henri Desgrange stands near the summit of the Col du Galibier, honouring his memory and his lifelong quest to make the Tour de France an elemental contest between man and nature.

For the 100th edition of the Tour in 2013 the race visited both Mont Ventoux and treated the fans with a double ascent of L'Alpe d'Huez on the same day during stage 18. Using a little used, tricky and narrow descent of the Col de Sarenne, on the other side of the ski station summit, the peloton returned to the climb for a thrilling finale, won by Christophe Riblon. In 2014, the Col d'Izoard featured on stage 14 and eventual race winner Vincenzo Nibali put the result beyond doubt when he won at the summit of Hautacam on stage 18.

Short, very steep climbs increasingly feature in modern Tours as they provoke exciting, attacking racing and dramatic time gaps, especially at or near the end of a stage, if the stage itself is around 150km or less. This has encouraged Tour route planners to go off in search of hitherto unheard-of climbs like the Mont du Chat in the Jura mountains, which the 2017 Tour crossed 25km from the finish of stage nine in Chambery. Notoriously steep, it is one of the hardest climbs in France and, as predicted, the race exploded on the way up. But it was on the wickedly sinuous descent that race favourite Richie Porte misjudged a corner, crashing heavily and leaving the race in the back of an ambulance.

There was another first in the 2017 Tour, when the venerable Col d'Izoard was chosen as the summit finish for stage 18, thrilling the fans as French stage winner Warren Barguil sped through the barren rock towers of La Casse Déserte before the triumphant final uphill to the summit finish line at 2,360m. In 2019 the mighty Col du Tourmalet hosted a summit finish, as did two other climbs above 2,000 metres: the climbs to Tignes and Val Thorens. The latter, its road summit at 2,365 metres, was only featuring in the Tour for the second time in 25 years.

Christian Prudhomme's bold inclusion of new climbs has proved to be a winner in every sense, and is no better exemplified by a six-kilometre "wall" in the Vosges mountains. La Planche des Belles Filles made its Tour debut in 2012 and has hosted stage finishes five times. Each has been significant to the race but in 2020 it decided the final result when Tadej Pogacar overturned a deficit of 57 seconds on yellow jersey-holder Primoz Roglic in the stage 20 time trial. Pogacar's sensational ride gave the 21-year-old an unassailable lead with only one day to go and guaranteed notoriety for the giant-killing hill.

THE GREAT CLIMBS

Just About the Bikes

The rider will always be the most important component, but that does not mean that his bicycle cannot affect the outcome of a race.

In motorsport it is universally accepted that the machine plays a crucial role in determining success or failure. A machine, such as a car or motorbike, is composed of hundreds of components, each one interacting with the others and having an influence on performance and handling. It's all about the agility of the machine, its power and its weight. In cycling all these things are relevant, but they apply so much more to the rider than the bike that the machine's importance is distinctly secondary in terms of its influence on the outcome of a race.

This is because the bicycle is one of the simplest and most efficient machines ever created. It has been around in its current form, with a diamond-shaped frame, wheels of equal size, and a chain-driven transmission, for more than a hundred years, and in that time has evolved into a reliable, fast, strong and lightweight device that can be improved upon only in tiny increments.

Even then, the advantages to be had can be measured only in fractions of seconds. No, the real machine in cycling is the rider – a complex jumble of physical attributes, contrasting skills, power and weight that propels the bicycle underneath him to victory, or defeat.

HANDY HANDLEBARS

That is not to say that the bike never plays its part in deciding the outcome of a race. When Greg LeMond wiped out a 50-second deficit on Laurent Fignon in the final time trial of the 1989 Tour de France he was undoubtedly helped by the use of an extension to his handlebars that brought his arms together in an aerodynamic ski tuck. The use of tri or aero bars is now established as the only way to ride a solo time trial, as it has been proven that they are seconds faster per kilometre than a

RIGHT: Bernard Hinault rides on the drops of his handlebars to improve his aerodynamics.

OPPOSITE ABOVE: A pre-1920s racer with a long wheelbase to cope with rough roads.

OPPOSITE BELOW: By the 1960s the racing bike had evolved into a multi-geared, lightweight machine.

conventional riding position. But the rider remains the most important element. On its own the aero bar does not make the bike faster: it's only when the rider narrows his frontal area while holding the bars that speed-sapping drag is reduced. Solid disc wheels, wafer-thin aerofoil frame tubes and concealed cables all contribute to reducing drag, but the position and shape of the rider is always the key factor when it comes to reducing the frontal area.

Showcasing the latest in bike technology has not always been the Tour's forte. Henri Desgrange's obsession with an equal contest between athletes led to the introduction in 1930 of a standard bike, painted yellow in the colours of *L'Auto*, and derailleur (originally dérailleur) gears, which had been used by touring cyclists since the 1920s, were not allowed to be used on the Tour until 1937. When the French firm Mavic produced an alloy rim in 1934, which was nearly half the weight of the

"Because of adverse weather conditions on the Croce d'Aune pass, Tullio Campagnolo conceived the idea to develop a quick-release mechanism for bicycle wheels."

CAMPAGNOLO

Campagnolo

Campagnolo is the most famous name in bicycles. Founded in 1933 in Vicenza, Italy, by former racer Tullio Campagnolo, the firm made its name with a quick-release lever that enabled a wheel to be removed in seconds. Legend had it that Tullio had come up with the idea after struggling to remove a wheel with frozen fingers at the top of a mountain pass. By the 1950s Campagnolo's Gran Sport derailleur was the first gear to use the parallelogram design that is still in use today, and by the 1960s most Tour riders and winners were riding with Campagnolo Nuovo Record gears and components. Campagnolo dominated professional cycling until the end of the last century, when the rapid acceptance of Shimano parts from Japan ended the Italian monopoly.

LEFT: Campagnolo isn't quite the dominant brand it was throughout the 20th century, but it remains one of the most iconic names in cycling.

OPPOSITE: Bradley Wiggins is the complete wind-cheating package with his domed aerodynamic time-trial helmet, flat-backed bent body position and Pinarello time-trial machine as he consolidates his 2012 Tour title with time-trial victory in Chartres.

BELOW: Electronic gears were universal in the 2020 peloton and after some resistance disc brakes are now commonplace.

steel version, they were banned, of course, but Antonin Magne successfully tried a pair at the Tour, painted to look like wooden racing rims.

Campagnolo's Grand Sport derailleur gear was, however, a revelation in the 1951 Tour, when it was used by the winner Hugo Koblet as well as Fausto Coppi and Gino Bartali. Bartali had been a skilled user of its forerunner, the Cambio Corsa derailleur, which involved several dextrous operations to effect a change, and won the 1938 Tour to confirm the success of the new device.

FASTER, STRONGER, LIGHTER

Over the next 40 years racing bikes improved in every area without ever changing their classic outline. Stronger and lighter steel tubing, better alloys and improved manufacturing techniques all contributed to a reliable racing machine not that far removed from the carbon fibre machines of today. Even now, there are pages of rules governing the design of a racing bike that can be used in the Tour, and bicycles that come in under the

Union Cycliste Internationale (UCI) weight limit of 6.8kg have to be weighed down with lead.

Much of the thinking behind modern advances to the bike is driven by aerodynamics. This has been the case since 1979 when Bernard Hinault rode a Tour time trial on his Gitane Delta bike, which had been tested in a wind tunnel. Painted in electric blue, the Delta had hidden cables and bladed tubes, bars and spokes. In 1984 Francesco Moser broke the hour record on a sensational-looking machine developed in the Pininfarina wind tunnel. Its disc wheels, low-slung bars and unconventional frame set the tone for the way-out track bikes ridden by the US team at the Los Angeles Olympic Games later that same year.

LeMond's aero bars sparked off the next stage of the revolution, which put more emphasis on the position of the rider, and this was taken to extremes by ingenious Scot Graeme Obree, whose hour record attempts in contorted riding positions in the 1990s proved a point but failed to convince the UCI that they would be anything but suicidal when tried outside of a track. Working within the rules,

Tour riders are in a constant process of refining their bikes, clothing and helmets, and it comes as something of a relief to know that among all this techno wizardry a Tour bicycle can still run over a thorn and get a puncture. As every incremental gain is sought, chicanery is a possibility too. At the 2010 Tour de France, bicycles were scanned by X-ray machines for hidden motors after time trial star Fabian Cancellara was accused of having a motor in his bicycle earlier that year.

The Tour is also an opportunity for bicycle and product manufacturers to show off their latest innovations. Modern racing has seen the advent of concealed brake blocks and electronic gears for even faster and more precise gear changes. Shimano's Di2 system was first used by riders in the 2009 race.

The most controversial innovation in recent years has been the introduction of hydraulic disc brakes into the pro peloton. Popular with hobby cyclists, and almost universal on mountain bikes, discs were only introduced on a trial basis in the late summer of 2015, but by spring of the following year the trial had been abruptly suspended after riders involved in pile-ups had apparently suffered cuts from discs. With much invested in mass production of disc brake-equipped machines, the industry worked hard on safety features with numerous pro teams expected to roll out on the new bikes with discs for the 2017 season.

One advantage of disc brakes is the extra clearance around the fork crown and rear stays, allowing the fitment of much fatter tyres than traditional sizes. Bigger tyres with a higher volume of air can be run at lower pressures for more comfort and no trade-off in rolling resistance. Tubular tyres, however, which require laborious gluing on to the rims, is one of the last jobs of the pro mechanic that has remained unchanged for more than 100 years.

Time Trials

Along with stages in the mountains, time trials are where the Tour is won and lost. Pitting yourself against the clock is known as "the race of truth".

Tour de France riders fear the time trials almost as much as they revere the mountain stages. For those riders fighting for an overall position, a time trial is where seconds and minutes are paid out to every competitor, ruthlessly allotting a ranking to each one and often resulting in a shuffling of the overall pack. From each one, riding alone over a set distance, with a ticking watch the only arbiter, the time trial demands a level of suffering equal to anything else on the bike. What is especially daunting is that the pain is self-imposed and self-regulated, which is not the same as suffering behind another's wheel or on a mountain pass. A wheel must be followed closely or you will be dropped from the pack, a mountain pass is a physical obstacle that must be overcome – neither carries the psychological torment that makes a time trial a true test of a rider's mental strength.

FORM INDICATOR

There are several different types of time trial in the modern Tour de France. All, apart from the team time trial, are run off with individual riders starting at set intervals, usually of two minutes. The prologue time trial, first introduced in 1967, is now the traditional curtain-opener to the Tour. Not usually classed as a stage, it is nevertheless an important indicator of the form and motivation of the leading riders. The race distance is short, between 5km and 10km, but occasionally longer, for example in 2000 when the prologue was 16.5km and because of its length was classed as a stage. Almost always the prologue takes place in the centre of the town hosting the Grand Départ, and the style of the course is designed to be fast, relatively flat and with

1989 drama

The most decisive and probably most exciting time trial ever seen in the Tour de France has to be one that resulted in the smallest overall winning margin in Tour history. Just eight seconds separated winner Greg LeMond from Laurent Fignon after stage 21 of the 1989 Tour, which broke with tradition by finishing with a 24.5km time trial in the centre of Paris. LeMond started the race 50 seconds behind Fignon, but the Frenchman could not contain the American, who used an innovative new aerodynamic handlebar extension to ride the race of his life and cause an upset from which Fignon's career never recovered. Aero, or tri-bars, quickly found their way on to every time trial bike. It is now accepted that without them a TT win is impossible.

BOTTOM LEFT: Antonin Magne races in the Tour's first ever time trial between La Roche-sur-Yon and Nantes in 1934.

RIGHT: Greg LeMond during the suspense-filled final stage of the 1989 Tour.

BELOW: Stephen Roche won the time trial from Saumur to Futuroscope and the 1987 Tour.

good accessibility for the many fans who descend en masse to see the Tourmen for the first time. It is not supposed to produce race-winning time gaps between the favourites either. Exceptions include the start of the 2005 Tour when, at 19km, the prologue was again too long to be classed as such, and the race from Fromentine to the island of Noirmoutier was not only spectator-unfriendly, it allowed Lance Armstrong to put more than a minute into his principal rivals for overall victory.

THE TOUR'S FIRST TIME TRIAL

It was in the same Vendée region that the Tour's first ever individual time trial, or *contre la montre* (against the watch), took place in 1934, held over an 83km course between La Roche-sur-Yon and Nantes and won by that

year's overall winner Antonin Magne. The result was significant and conclusive evidence that a Tour winner must also win time trials, or at the very least finish consistently high on every time trial stage. Many Tour winners in the years that followed increasingly used superior time trialling abilities to build and consolidate their campaigns for the overall classification.

As the era of the heroic lone breakaway across all types of terrain began to fade, thanks to more tightly controlled bunch racing and higher levels of ability throughout the peloton, the time trial in effect took the place of the lone break. It remains a link to the Tour de France as envisioned by Tour founder Henri Desgrange, who wanted the race to be a contest between individuals riding without team assistance or any form of pacing.

ABOVE: Lunch time on the Tour for Edward Vissers, Albert Perikel and Albertin Disseaux during the 1939 race.

> "There are two principal attributes of a Tour winner: the strength to ride a long time trial and the endurance to ride the steep mountain ascents."
>
> *USA TODAY*

ABOVE: Australia's Rohan Dennis is the current holder of the fastest average speed in a solo Tour time trial.

OPPOSITE: Primoz Roglic lost the yellow jersey with one day to go in the 2020 Tour stage 20 time trial.

RIGHT: White jersey leader Rein Taaramae goes uphill during the 2012 Tour time-trial between Arc-et-Senans and Besançon.

Modern Tours typically have two time trials, roughly 50km in length, positioned in the first and third weeks, with the mountain stages in between. There have been many variations, however, with a team time trial sometimes included in place of at least one of the solo time trials, while shorter but always decisive mountain time trials provide an opportunity for the lightly built climbers who lack horsepower on the flat and can be seriously disadvantaged in long time trials on flat or rolling roads. Time trialling is essentially a test of speed, and the sleek machines with carbon fibre wheels, piloted by riders in pointed, aerodynamic helmets, also make it one of the most spectacular elements of the Tour. To the roadside spectator a time trial stage is the Tour at its most accessible and offering the best value – half a day of action, with every member of the peloton passing by, easily identified in the pages of *L'Equipe* and just a few metres away.

While dominance in time trials has underpinned Tour de France triumphs for the likes of Jacques Anquetil and Miguel Indurain, the best men against the clock are not always wannabe race winners. Fabian Cancellara is one of the finest exponents of the art of time trialling. An Olympic champion in the discipline in 2008 and 2016, the powerful and fluid Swiss rider won his first prologue time trial in Liège in 2004 and added wins in three more prologues and three long Tour time trials. Those have contributed to him spending 29 days in the yellow jersey, but his hefty 80kg frame means he loses the race lead as soon as the race hits the first stiff mountain.

Much kudos is placed on the holder of the fastest time trial in the Tour de France. Since 1994 the record was held by British champion Chris Boardman, averaging 55.2kph during the 7.2km prologue in Lille and it took a phenomenal performance by Australian Rohan Dennis to increase the record speed to 55.446kph over almost twice the distance, 13.8km, on a flat course around the streets of Utrecht in 2015. Not surprisingly both riders had track backgrounds and were one-time holders of the World Hour Record. Incidentally the prologue of the 2015 Tour was the only individual time trial of the race, with just a team time trial over 28km on stage nine. This represented a trend in recent Tours favouring shorter mountain stages and summit finales, designed to add excitement and, hopefully, keep the results in doubt until the end of the third week of racing. Gone were the long individual time trials of earlier editions of the Tour when a favourite could destroy his rivals over 50km and effectively kill the race long before the final week.

When a shorter time trial is combined with a steep uphill finish, fireworks are usually guaranteed, and never was that more the case than in 2020 when a 36km time trial finishing up the Planche des Belles Filles climb delivered one of the most sensational upsets in Tour history. Yellow jersey-holder Primoz Roglic was widely expected to hold or even increase his lead, but there was nothing he could do about Slovenian compatriot Tadej Pogacar, who obliterated his lead and snatched yellow with just one day to go.

Sponsored Teams

A professional cyclist is a pedalling billboard with every visible part of his clothing and equipment hired out to sponsors, all of whom want to be seen by the biggest global audience for a cycling event.

Cycling and marketing make ideal, though quaint, bedfellows. The transaction is simple – a commercial enterprise pays to have its name printed on a jersey which is then seen by the general public by the roadside and on television. It is an exercise in product awareness, the most benign form of unhip advertising, long since outmoded by the in-your-face hard sell, the sneaky subliminal and the fear factor. The principle is that you see a brand name, associate it with your favourite sport and then, just maybe, buy the product. Cycling makes marketing look like an innocent activity, and the Tour de France proves beyond argument that soft selling can work if you make it entertaining, aspirational and fun.

BACKERS BIG AND SMALL

Nearly two hundred riders representing 22 teams line up for the start of a modern Tour. Most have at least two prominent sponsors on their clothing, and there are often dozens of other branded parts and named backers elsewhere on bikes and other riding kit such as helmets, shoes and glasses. That adds up to hundreds of sponsors for the teams alone; add in 40 of the Tour's official partners and nearly 50 organisations in the publicity

caravan and the message is chaotic but undeniably colourful.

ASO is the private organisation which runs the Tour, unlike football's World Cup or the Olympic movement. It is now separate from L'Équipe, the newspaper which succeeded L'Auto as race organiser. It is inconceivable that the Tour could operate without the support of independent teams, the publicity caravan, race partners and, of course, the TV rights on which everything must turn. It has not always been that way. Between 1930 and 1961 the Tour was contested by national teams, and it was again in 1967–68 when they were reintroduced for a short period in an attempt to curtail the influence of the sponsors, and create a great contest between nations similar to the Olympics and World Cup. This was the intention of Tour founder Henri Desgrange, who introduced the national team format in 1930. But as with the genesis of the Tour itself, there was a lot more to the enterprise than Corinthian ideals of sportsmanship.

Desgrange was never comfortable with the influence that the bicycle industry had over the riders in his early Tours. La Française, Peugeot and Alcyon were all team winners of Tours between 1903 and 1929, and despite the huge popularity of the race through

LEFT: BMC team-mates George Hincapie (left) and Michael Schär work hard to position BMC team leader Cadel Evans (behind) on stage 13 of the 2012 Tour between Saint-Paul-Trois-Châteaux and Cap d'Agde – and keep the sponsor's name highly visible.

OPPOSITE TOP LEFT: The Tour de France in the 1930s sometimes took on the appearance of a village fête. Liqueur manufacturer Cointreau created masks of three of the most popular cyclists of this era, André Leducq, Roger Lapébie and Charles Pélissier, and Leducq and Péllissier's are here.

OPPOSITE BELOW: Team Jumbo-Visma dominated the 2020 Tour de France, with three stage wins and a long spell in the yellow jersey.

RIGHT: Every space for sale – cotton throwaway food bags, "Musettes", advertise supermarkets Spar and Coop.

the 1920s Desgrange was irritated by the lack of French winners during that time and dismayed by a team ethic that he felt was contrary to the noble ideal of lone riders competing against each other with no outside assistance whatsoever. His reforms worked, up to a point, bringing about the return of French winners in the 1930s, but also confirming that massed-start cycle racing between teams was an inevitable development of the sport.

From 1969 the Tour has been contested by sponsored teams. Faema, an Italian maker of espresso coffee machines, won the prize for best team and was also the name on the jersey and shorts of the Belgian winner of the 1969 Tour, Eddy Merckx. All the riders on Merckx's team were Belgian, which might have given Desgrange a grim sense of satisfaction from beyond the grave. When cycling became an international sport, in the 1980s, sponsored teams with riders from one nation would become very scarce indeed.

145

Gitane

Gitane bicycles have been ridden to 11 Tour wins, and the French cigarette manufacturer has a long and glorious history of sponsorship, most notably of Jacques Anquetil in the 1960s and Bernard Hinault and Laurent Fignon in the 1970s and 80s. This was the heyday of the first superteam of the modern era, Renault-Gitane, under the astute management of Cyrille Guimard. After guiding Lucien Van Impe (right) to his one and only Tour win in 1976 (on a Gitane), Renault bought out Gitane and in 1977 brought together the cream of French cyclists with a budget that exceeded all others. In 1981 Greg LeMond and Jonathan Boyer became the first two riders from the USA to join a Tour de France-winning team, setting the scene for the English-speaking revolution that was to transform the sport throughout the 1980s.

MODERN SPONSORSHIP

Professional cycling teams in the twenty-first century are essentially run along the same lines as the Tour teams from 30 years earlier. Most have a pyramid structure to their sponsorship, with a single main backer at the top putting in the bulk of the funding while more numerous partners lower

ABOVE: Having a Tour de France stage winner like André Greipel showing your logo on the podium is good for business.

BELOW: Team Sky at the pinnacle of cycling, on the final podium of the Tour celebrating Chris Froome's third victory, and the team's fourth.

146

"The Postal Service and Lance took a sport that was relatively unknown in America and put it into everyone's homes, businesses and lives."

FRANKIE ANDREU, US POSTAL RIDER

down pay less or supply the team with the material to do the job.

Budgets are counted in the millions, and the British-backed Team Sky was rated as the most expensive team of all time with a budget of more than £24m for the 2015 season. A budget pays for much more than a three-week trip to the Tour de France with nine riders. It has to cover a year's wages for 30 cyclists, a manager plus on-the-road *directeurs sportifs*, mechanics, physios and *soigneurs* (masseurs), doctors and physicians and bus drivers.

There are travel costs during the racing season between February and October, cars and equipment vans, plus big bills for fitting out and running the team bus and providing facilities. Team Sky's wage bill alone (£18m) was more than the total running costs of just about every other team in the World Tour.

Team Sky's, now Ineos Grenadiers, recruitment policy, finding the best people for the many diverse roles on a pro cycling team, is the envy of every other team, and while others may not have as much to spend, it has led to a culture shift in the way modern teams are run. Ineos Grenadiers' budget has increased by about £15 million since its debut in 2010, and that reflects the positive return on seven Tour de France and multiple other racing successes leading to an estimated $550 million in marketing value.

Ineos Grenadiers and its partner sponsors, which include Pinarello bikes and Castelli clothing, all take an interest in which races and countries the team competes in, and even the nationality of riders they contract. But a good showing at the Tour de France remains by far the most important return on their investment.

LEFT: German team T-Mobile was one of the best-funded teams of the modern era.

147

SPONSORED TEAMS

The Directeurs Sportifs

Every team has a manager: not a backroom administrator, but a director of sports who follows the team by car and co-ordinates the race strategy.

Behind every Tour winner there is a team, and behind every team there is a *directeur sportif*. The *domestiques*, the star riders, the race programme and race battle plan are all the responsibility of the *directeur sportif*, who is, in effect, the general of a miniature army which mobilises each July to engage in the war of the Tour. A good Tour means different things to different teams but one thing is certain: even a modicum of success can lift the fortunes of a team, whether they are looking to hang on to a sponsor, contract a leading rider or turn around a barren season. And it is the *directeur sportif* to whom everyone turns when it comes to setting goals for the Tour squad and, what's more important, implementing a strategy to achieve them.

A YEAR IN THE MAKING

The road to winning the Tour de France begins 12 months before each edition, when the *directeur sportif* during that year's Tour either confirms the contracts of riders already on his Tour team, or makes serious approaches to star riders on other teams. Whatever happens during the Tour, the "DS" will already be thinking about the possible make-up of the squad when the Tour reconvenes a year up the road. The team will not change between the end of July and the end of the year and there will be many more races to ride, often including another three-

week national tour in Spain, the Vuelta, but the game plan for the following year's campaign, starting with team bonding exercises in the winter, then training camps before the racing starts again in February, will take up much of the DS's time. He will delegate his assistant *directeurs* to manage the team in lesser events while concentrating on ensuring that the business plan is on track.

DOWN TO BUSINESS

A modern professional cycling team is run as a business and, unlike a football club, where the manager is an employee of the club, many *directeurs sportifs* actually own or are part-owners of the teams they manage. The name of the company that owns the team will not appear on the jerseys or shorts of the riders – that space is reserved for sponsors or "associates" of the company who might be paying millions of Euros for the privilege of having their name in the team's headline but have little or no influence on the running of the outfit itself. The DS-owner is a powerful individual in cycling, and one whose influence on the sport can be traced through what is basically one team which over the years has confusingly been known by the names of a number of unrelated top-line sponsors. A good example is the French DS Roger Legeay, a former professional who has managed, in effect,

FAR LEFT: Jan Janssen is deafened by his manager during the tense final time trial of the 1968 Tour. The Dutchman won overall by 38 seconds.

NEAR LEFT: Former rider, now *directeur sportif* Cyrille Guimard (right, with Laurent Fignon) knew what it was like to struggle on a mountain stage of the Tour.

OPPOSITE: Chris Froome celebrates his first Tour victory in 2013, toasting his sport directors in the Team Sky car with a glass of fizz.

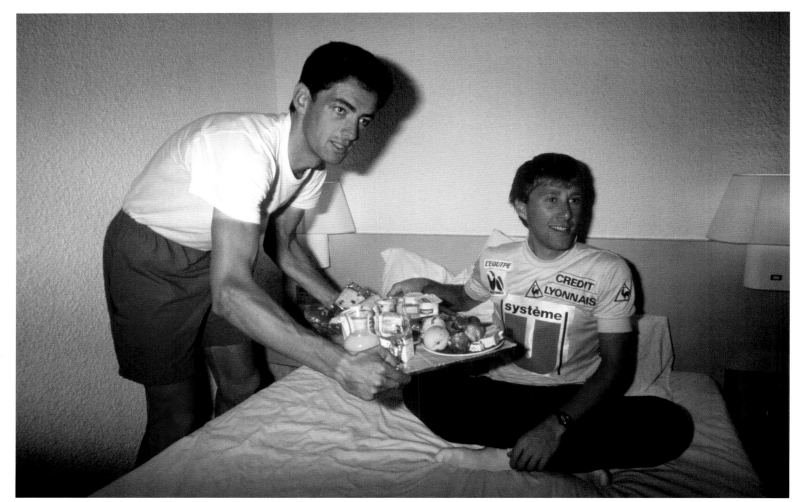

TOP: Race leader Charly Mottet relaxes in bed on a rest day during the 1987 Tour while team-mate Marc Madiot supplies breakfast in bed. In charge of the FDJ team, Madiot has gone on to become one of the most respected *directeurs sportifs* in the pack.

LEFT: David Moncoutié of the Cofidis team (left) with his *directeur sportif* Eric Boyer.

the same team from 1988, known successively as Peugeot (cars and bikes), "Z" (children's clothing), Gan (insurance), and Crédit Agricole (bank).

When teams were smaller the *directeur sportif* might have had a hand in the coaching of riders and the general day-to-day running of the outfit. Nowadays most teams have assistants and coaches who train the riders, and there will be an office which takes care of all the travel and accommodation headaches. One job that remains central to the role of the DS, however, is that of motivating the team and organising them from a following car during the race. In the Tour he will travel in the team car, in a long line of all the rival team vehicles, with the one belonging to the leading team in the race following directly behind the bunch, that of the second team next, and so on down to the 22nd team. In the team car, usually a diesel-powered family estate, every glovebox and available space on the dashboard is taken up with communications equipment and a screen showing live TV images of the race. From here the DS can communicate directly with all of his riders in the peloton via radio earpieces. Teams have always been controlled by the *directeur sportif*, and the revolution in telecoms has enabled him to see more and react faster than ever before. Gone are the days when the only way to communicate with a rider was by means of a dangerous drive up the line of the cars into the back of the bunch. Now, the all-seeing, all-powerful DS wields more influence on the pattern of racing in the Tour than ever before.

Although it is now accepted that radio earpieces are just another tool of the trade, it has almost certainly resulted in tactics which can be predictable with manoeuvres orchestrated by a disembodied voice in the team car. Some riders, Thomas

ABOVE: World champion Mark Cavendish (left) gets a mechanical fix on the fly and talks tactics with his *directeur sportif* Sean Yates.

BELOW: Team Sky sports director Sean Yates pats Bradley Wiggins on the back following his 2012 Tour victory.

> **"When a rider is under pressure it's impossible to think of more than four or five things. My job is to think ahead on their behalf."**
> *NICOLAS PORTAL, TEAM SKY SPORTS DIRECTOR*

Voeckler for instance, famously eschewed instructions from his sport manager and raced on instinct alone. That's fine for the maverick but it does not fit with the highly organised and well-drilled team effort that is required to win a modern Tour de France.

Team Sky's three Tour de France wins were built on meticulous pre-race planning and familiarity with every key feature of each stage. Long gone are the days when riders and *directeurs sportifs* would peruse the next day's stage over dinner the night before. Today's sports directors are multi-tasking heroes, making tactical decisions in a fast-changing environment, warning their riders of key features along the route, all this while helming a team car inches from other team cars and crazy pro riders!

151

THE DIRECTEURS SPORTIFS

Sean Yates

Sean Yates was a respected rider in the 1980s and 1990s, wearing the yellow jersey in the 1994 Tour. He also gained a reputation as a rapid descender, and as an eccentric for his earrings and vegetarianism. The Briton went on to manage Lance Armstrong alongside Johan Bruyneel at Discovery Channel in 2005, but his first Tour de France win as chief manager was behind the wheel of the Team Sky car for Bradley Wiggins in 2012. Yates has an old-school sangfroid and an impassive, analytical attitude to race action, enabling him to reach detached tactical decisions. While his experience and knowledge make him a valuable member of Team Sky, his no-nonsense style and dry post-race assessments make him popular with the press and public.

The Publicity Caravan

If the yellow jersey is the emblem of the Tour, the publicity caravan is the blaring fanfare that precedes its arrival. The Tour would not be the same without it.

CUSTOMS AND TRADITIONS

Love it or hate it, the *caravane publicitaire* is part of the fabric of the Tour de France which, without it, would begin to resemble any other major bike race. Consisting of 170 vehicles representing 43 organisations, the publicity caravan arrives at least one hour in advance of the race itself and over the course of three weeks hands out more than 14 million gifts. To approximately 15 million roadside spectators the caravan signals the start of the build-up to the arrival of the Tour. To the many children dragged along by their parents the publicity caravan is much more exciting than the peloton flashing by an hour later.

ATTENTION GRABBING

Many of the vehicles in the caravan are custom-built and painted to attract maximum attention. Leaning out of every open top and standing on running boards are hardy youngsters who brave all weathers to throw out paper hats, sweets, plastic bags and key rings to anyone and everyone at the roadside. They start the race quite pale and cheerful, and arrive in Paris with dark suntans and a stoical smile on their faces. French business overwhelmingly supports the publicity caravan, with names like Café Grand Mère, Haribo, Kléber, La Vache Qui Rit, Nesquik, PMU and Le Journal de Mickey appealing to young and old alike. The French army, police and fire service are also represented, as are some of the Tour's official sponsors such as Skoda and

"The Tour de France isn't just a bike race. It's a huge moving show and the caravan is a vital part of it."

ARNAUD COLLAS, AQUAREL MARKETING MANAGER

152

LEFT: Before the real business of the race, the atmosphere often resembles something between a local festival and a village fête. Under the scorching sun, hats, such as those given out by the the newspaper *L'Auto* (left) and the mustard producer Amora (right) were simultaneously prized memorabilia and useful protection.

Festina. Not only do they make up a colourful and promo carrier bag-filling spectacle; the caravan can also be heard from many kilometres away as it transmits tinny music and hoarse exhortations at ear-splitting decibels. Noisy, polluting, vulgar, fun. That is the point of the caravan and the Tour makes no apology for it. Today's caravan is marshalled by the French Gendarmerie and must pay particular attention to the very real danger and sometimes tragic consequences of children running into the road.

The publicity caravan was created by the Tour founder Henri Desgrange in 1930, based on an idea of M Paul Thévenin of chocolate-makers Menier, a race partner. The companies

assumed part of the expenses of travel for the national and regional teams, the other innovation for the 1930 Tour. Desgrange wanted to remove the problems caused by the operation of the teams since 1903, specifically the preeminence of the manufacturers' cycles. It also sought to be a means of supporting the French riders who had not won the Tour since Henri Pélissier in 1923. Glowing in the patriotic upsurge caused by the success of the Davis Cup tennis team's "the Four Musketeers", Desgrange thus invited five teams of eight champions, representing France, Belgium, Italy, Spain and Germany. He also invited 60 regional riders to add local colour to this revolutionary concept.

LEFT: Pento hair products came for the ride in the 1954 Tour.

BELOW: Some items that emerge from the caravan, like this Martini fan, are highly collectable.

BELOW: Strange and unusual vehicles, like this Dan Dare-style BiC car from 1955, were guaranteed to fascinate and amuse.

RIGHT: Cheap gifts, like this keyring, are scattered like confetti by the publicity caravan.

OPPOSITE: Perrier water were long-time supporters of the race and a welcome freebie during long hot stages.

153

THE PUBLICITY CARAVAN

THE CARAVAN'S CREATION

All were to ride identical bicycles, painted yellow, to ensure that no mechanical advantage could be gained and also to prevent famous bike names profiting from exposure in the Tour. To help fund the race in the absence of trade teams and to give commercial interests a neutral platform in the race, Desgrange created the *caravane publicitaire*, which quickly grew to become a staple of the Tour. When trade teams returned to the Tour in the 1960s and 70s the caravan suffered as money moved from one to the other. France's ban on cigarette and alcohol advertising has also lost some familiar names from the caravan. Over the years convoy stalwarts included the motorbike-riding Michelin men

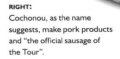

and the Catch fly-spray vehicle with a huge fibreglass fly upside down on the roof!

The majority of the six hundred people who work on the modern Tour caravan are students or young people, seeing France on a summer job. While the passing vehicles provide the spectacle, the reaction of the viewing public is a sight to behold too. Grown men and women wait with hands on thighs like cricketers waiting for a slip catch as the vehicles approach, and competition sometimes turns into scraps for the thrown items. Well, everyone loves a freebie and few go away disappointed or empty-handed from the mêlée. The publicity caravan has become an integral part of a spectator's day out.

Although they are not officially part of the publicity caravan there are hundreds of other vehicles which precede the Tour and which also attract much interest, support and sometimes booing from the crowds. Official Tour vehicles, bristling with aerials and painted blue or red, the police outriders on their motorbikes, plus press motorbikes and press cars create constant interest as knowledgeable fans crane their necks to catch sight of a famous, or infamous, ex-rider who has joined the press corps or is in an official race vehicle. Team cars in support roles might also run ahead of the race and are always welcomed with a cheer, or a jeer.

The modern *caravane publicitaire* is just as noisy and crazy as it ever was, but with GPS and additional health and safety concerns, it's more thoroughly managed than ever before. The young people on the outside of the floats wear harnesses, and each vehicle can be tracked with GPS. That's important because the whole procession can cover up to 20km of the stage route. It can take 35 minutes for the caravan to trundle past while the music blares and souvenir items are thrown out to the crowd. It's not unusual, especially on flatter stages, for large numbers of roadside "fans" to fill their pockets with keyrings and sweets and return happily to their cars before the race has arrived!

OPPOSITE: The figures may be modern but the tradition remains the same. It works for the millions of bounty hunters who throng the road as the Tour caravan rumbles by.

ABOVE: Classic Citroën 2CVs and hardy girls of the caravan provide pre-race fun before the 1992 Tour.

RIGHT: Cochonou, as the name suggests, make pork products and "the official sausage of the Tour".

BELOW: Nestlé's huge Aquarel promotion at the 2001 Tour ultimately paid off.

Getting Noticed

Nestlé launched a new brand of bottled water, Aquarel, at the 2001 Tour, spending approximately one franc per spectator on a three-week campaign centred on the publicity caravan. Motorised bottles of Aquarel, free bottles of Aquarel and firemen and clowns all promoted the new brand during their three-week marathon in the publicity caravan. Nestlé gave away 500,000 bottles of Aquarel during the 2001 Tour de France but it was probably worth the effort and expense as they were able to record a 50 per cent increase in sales after the 2001 launch.

155

THE PUBLICITY CARAVAN

L'Arrivée Finale

Paris rarely hosts the start of the modern Tour de France, but the finish is now firmly established as a high-speed victory parade in the centre of the capital.

Paris has always been the destination, or actual location, of the final stage of the Tour de France. The first Tour in 1903 finished in Ville d'Avray in the south-west suburbs of Paris, near to a café called "Le Père Auto" – but with no connection to the newspaper *L'Auto* – and not far from the Parc des Princes track at the Porte de St Cloud, where the riders were paraded in front of a huge crowd after the stage finish. The Parc des Princes track, an open-air 666.66m banked oval, was built in 1897 and selected by Tour founder Henri Desgrange as the ideal place to finish the Tour, which occurred without exception until 1971. The track was indeed a great choice, as it was big enough to hold a large crowd and the shallow bankings and long straights could be easily ridden by the exhausted Tourmen on their road bikes. In the first two years of the race the field had to complete a 460km stage, starting from Nantes, before arriving in Paris, and these two stages remain the longest ever final legs of the Tour.

A FINAL FLOURISH

For the next 30 years the Tour arrived at the Parc des Princes, many times from a northerly port such as Dunkirk, having covered at least 300km before the welcome sight of the track hove into view. In 1932 the distance was reduced to 159km and the packed trackside crowd were treated to an exciting sprint win by French yellow jersey and overall winner André Leducq. From then until 1964 the race to the track was over 200km but

"It feels really good to get to Paris. You can't wear yellow and win stages every year but I felt great out there today. I hardly touched the pedals."
STUART O'GRADY, 2006

ABOVE: July 1938, revered veterans and double Tour winners, André Leducq and Antonin Magne, bid masterly farewells by finishing side-by-side. Gino Bartali won his first Tour.

LEFT: Until 1967 the Parc des Princes hosted the finish of the Tour and a big crowd, like this one in 1930, was always guaranteed.

ABOVE: Share certificate for the Parc des Princes in Paris. The holder was given vouchers for free admission to a number of events held at the stadium.

TOP RIGHT: On the back of each ticket is a map of the Parc des Princes and the surrounding streets.

RIGHT: The Arc de Triomphe is an imposing backdrop to the final stage.

BELOW: The final day is not always a procession. Race winner Bernard Hinault had to mark attacking rival Joop Zoetemelk at the end of the 1979 Tour before winning to seal victory.

Sprint Finish

One of the most dramatic final stages on the Champs-Elysées took place in 1979, when the Dutchman Joop Zoetemelk, lying in second place, attacked on the run-in to Paris and was joined by the man wearing yellow, Bernard Hinault. The Frenchman was at the height of his powers and heading for the second of his five Tour wins, but felt he had to counter Zoetemelk's aggressive but crowd-pleasing move. The two of them found themselves ahead of the field, whereupon the impulsive Hinault thought "Why not?" and collaborated with the hapless Dutchman all the way to the line, where he delivered the coup de grâce by out-sprinting him.

FINISH OF THE TOUR DE FRANCE

Year(s)	Finish
1903	Ville d'Avray, Île-de-France
1904–1967	Parc des Princes, Paris
1968–1974	Vélodrome La Cipale, Bois de Vincennes
1975–present	Champs-Elysées, Paris

"Every sprinter dreams of putting their hands up in the air as they cross that line seeing the Arc de Triomphe in the foreground."

MARK CAVENDISH

rarely above 300km and stage starts remained in the north with places like Caen, Dieppe and Roubaix – whose velodrome is still used for the final laps of the great spring classic Paris–Roubaix.

As the Tour began to move away from the far corners of France, the 1950s saw final stages starting south of Paris in towns such as Dijon, Tours and Vichy.

In 1964 for the first time the Tour ended with a time trial on the final stage, from Versailles to the Parc des Princes. Jacques Anquetil, the French four-time winner of the race, was already in yellow, but he made sure of victory in the 27.5km test and was hailed as the first rider to win the Tour five times. With TV covering the entire race for the first time, the placing of a time trial at the end of the Tour, especially one with ace soloist Anquetil, was deemed a success. Time was running out for the Parc des Princes, however, and the venerable old track was demolished after Raymond Poulidor of France won the final time trial there at the end of the 1967 Tour de France.

The Tour moved to the La Cipale outdoor track in Vincennes on the south-east side of Paris, where it stayed until 1975. A final stage time trial continued until 1971 when, after three

years of consecutive stage and overall wins by Eddy Merckx, the Arrivée Finale reverted to a mass-start road race. It had no effect on the outcome though, with Merckx again achieving overall victory after the 89km stage from Versailles to Paris-La Cipale was won by Willy Teirlinck of Belgium. A year later the Tour finished in the centre of Paris on the most famous boulevard in France, the Champs-Elysées. It has stayed there ever since, the riders arriving in the centre of Paris and racing for an hour or so up and down the 2km cobbled stretch of *la plus belle avenue du monde* (the most beautiful avenue in the world). At 60 metres above sea level, the Arc de Triomphe at one end does not even merit fourth category status in the Tour's hill ranking classification. However, after three weeks of racing the high-speed finale stretches the weary peloton to near breaking point up the long drag from the Place de la Concorde to the Place Charles de Gaulle where the Arc is located. This is where the Tour exacts its final moments of true suffering. Only once since 1975 has the Tour run a time trial in place of a road race. In 1989 yellow jersey Laurent Fignon of France and the USA's Greg LeMond fought out a scintillating

24.5km time trial which finished on the Champs-Elysées in a nail biting finale. Fignon finally lost the Tour by eight seconds, the narrowest margin ever recorded.

Whether it was because of the shock of a Frenchman coming so close to victory, or the impossibility of ever re-creating such a close finish, the Tour since then has reverted to a ceremonial procession into Paris, followed by an acceleration on to the Champs-Elysées, leading up to one of the most highly prized sprint finishes in cycling.

Parisian specialist

Few men have won more than once on the Champs-Elysées, but Mark Cavendish has turned victory on the famous boulevard into a habit. The prolific British sprinter is the man who has won most often there, claiming four consecutive stage victories from 2009 to 2012. As the final stage is usually both short and relaxed in nature, it often presents a straightforward sprint. It is a perfect test for Cavendish, set up by helpers and able to burn off riders with his peerless turn of speed. His first win in 2009 was the most impressive. His victory margin was so emphatic that his trusted pilot, Mark Renshaw, had the time and space to finish second behind him.

BELOW: Sprint star Mark Cavendish is metres away from his second win in Paris, ahead of rival Alessandro Petacchi (green, behind) in the 2010 Tour.

OPPOSITE: Ouch: the painful moment that green jersey Djamolidine Abdoujaparov's trajectory is halted by a roadside barrier, metres from the finish line of the 1991 Tour.

BOTTOM: Behind their masks (left to right), Primoz Roglic, Tadej Pogacar and Richie Porte stand atop the 2020 Tour de France podium. A surreal scene to conclude a unique Tour.

L'ARRIVÉE FINALE

Records and Statistics

With more than 115 years of history, the Tour de France is a treasure trove of facts and figures. Every year, the three weeks of racing produce a forest of statistics, from individual stage winners to leaders of the classifications – ranging from the overall race leader to the best climber and team. Over multiple editions, records are set and broken as the rich tapestry of the Tour rolls ever on in to the future.

LEFT: Classification winners of the 2016 Tour (L to R): Britain's Adam Yates (best young rider) and Chris Froome (overall winner); Slovakian Peter Sagan (points winner); and Poland's Rafal Majka (best climber).

How the Tour Has Evolved...

The first Tour was in 1903. From 1905–12, victory was decided by points, the lowest scorer winning. In 1913, the Tour returned to timings, with the overall leader's *maillot jaune* first seen in 1919. The King of the Mountains (KoM) arrived in 1933, but the polka dot jersey came only in 1975. The green jersey points competition (Pts), decided by placings during each day's racing, started in 1953.

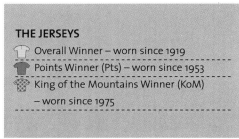

THE JERSEYS

Overall Winner – worn since 1919

Points Winner (Pts) – worn since 1953

King of the Mountains Winner (KoM) – worn since 1975

Le Tour 1903 (2428km)

July 1–July 21, Paris–Paris

1. Maurice Garin (FRA)	94hrs-33mins-14secs
2. Lucien Pothier (FRA)	+2-49-45
3. Fernand Augereau (FRA)	+4-29-38

Le Tour 1904 (2420km)

July 2–July 24, Paris–Paris

1. Henri Cornet (FRA)	96-05-55
2. Jean-Baptiste Dortignacq (FRA)	+2-16-14
3. Alois Catteau (FRA)	+8-07-20

Le Tour 1905 (2994km)

July 9–July 30, Paris–Paris

1. Louis Trousselier (FRA)	35 PTS
2. Hippolyte Aucouturier (FRA)	61 PTS
3. Jean-Baptiste Dortignacq (FRA)	64 PTS

Le Tour 1906 (4545km)

July 4–July 29, Paris–Paris

1. René Pottier (FRA)	31 PTS
2. Georges Passerieu (FRA)	45 PTS
3. Louis Trousselier (FRA)	59 PTS

Le Tour 1907 (4488km)

July 8–August 4, Paris–Paris

1. Lucien Petit-Breton (FRA)	47 PTS
2. Gustave Garrigou (FRA)	66 PTS
3. Emile Georget (FRA)	74 PTS

Le Tour 1908 (4488km)

July 13–August 9, Paris–Paris

1. Lucien Petit-Breton (FRA)	36 PTS
2. François Faber (LUX)	68 PTS
3. Georges Passerieu (FRA)	75 PTS

Le Tour 1909 (4497km)

July 5–August 1, Paris–Paris

1. François Faber (LUX)	37 PTS
2. Gustave Garrigou (FRA)	57 PTS
3. Jean Alavoine (FRA)	66 PTS

Le Tour 1910 (4737km)

July 3–July 31, Paris–Paris

1. Octave Lapize (FRA)	63 PTS
2. François Faber (LUX)	67 PTS
3. Gustave Garrigou (FRA)	86 PTS

Le Tour 1911 (5344km)

July 2–July 30, Paris–Paris

1. Gustave Garrigou (FRA)	43 PTS
2. Paul Duboc (FRA)	63 PTS
3. Emile Georget (FRA)	84 PTS

Le Tour 1912 (5289km)

June 30–July 28, Paris–Paris

1. Odile Defraye (BEL)	49 PTS
2. Eugène Christophe (FRA)	108 PTS
3. Gustave Garrigou (FRA)	140 PTS

Le Tour 1913 (5287km)

June 29–July 27, Paris–Paris

1. Philippe Thys (BEL)	197-54-00
2. Gustave Garrigou (FRA)	+8-37
3. Marcel Buysse (BEL)	+3-30-55

Le Tour 1914 (5380km)

June 28–July 26, Paris–Paris

1. Philippe Thys (BEL)	200-28-49
2. Henri Pelissier (FRA)	+1-40
3. Jean Alavoine (FRA)	+36-53

Le Tour 1919 (5560km)

June 29–July 27, Paris–Paris

1. Firmin Lambot (BEL)	231-07-15
2. Jean Alavoine (FRA)	+1-43-54
3. Eugène Christophe (FRA)	+2-16-31

Le Tour 1920 (5503km)

June 27–July 28, Paris–Paris

1. Philippe Thys (BEL)	228-36-13
2. Hector Heusghem (BEL)	+57-21
3. Firmin Lambot (BEL)	+1-39-35

Le Tour 1921 (5485km)

June 26–July 24, Paris–Paris

1. Léon Scieur (BEL)	221-50-00
2. Hector Heusghem (BEL)	+18-36
3. Honoré Barthélemy (FRA)	+2-01-00

Le Tour 1922 (5375km)

June 25–July 23, Paris–Paris

1. Firmin Lambot (BEL)	222-08-06
2. Jean Alavoine (FRA)	+41-15
3. Félix Sellier (FRA)	+42-02

Le Tour 1923 (5386km)

June 24–July 22, Paris–Paris

1. Henri Pelissier (FRA)	222-15-30
2. Ottavio Bottechia (ITA)	+30-41
3. Romain Bellenger (FRA)	+1-04-43

Le Tour 1924 (5425km)

June 22–July 20, Paris–Paris

1. Ottavio Bottechia (ITA)	226-18-21
2. Nicolas Frantz (LUX)	+35-36
3. Lucien Buysse (BEL)	+1-32-13

Le Tour 1925 (5440km)

June 21–July 19, Paris–Paris

1. Ottavio Bottechia (ITA)	219-10-18
2. Lucien Buysse (BEL)	+54-20
3. Bartolomeo Aymo (ITA)	+56-17

Le Tour 1926 (5745km)

June 20–July 18, Paris–Paris

1. Lucien Buysse (BEL)	238-44-25
2. Nicolas Frantz (LUX)	+1-22-25
3. Bartolomeo Aymo (ITA)	+1-22-51

Le Tour 1927 (5340km)

June 19–July 27, Paris–Paris

1. Nicolas Frantz (LUX)	198-16-42
2. Maurice Dewaele (BEL)	+1-48-21
3. Julien Vervaecke (BEL)	+2-25-06

HOW THE TOUR HAS EVOLVED...

LEFT: Belgium's Firmin Lambot (Bel) was a Tour winner in both 1919 and again in 1922.

164

Le Tour 1928 (5476km)

June 17–July 15, Paris–Paris

1. Nicolas Frantz (LUX)	👕	192-48-58
2. André Leducq (FRA)		+50-07
3. Maurice Dewaele (BEL)		+56-16

Le Tour 1929 (5257km)

June 30–July 28, Paris–Paris

1. Maurice Dewaele (BEL)	👕	186-39-16
2. Giuseppe Pancera (ITA)		+44-23
3. Joseph Demuysère (BEL)		+57-10

Le Tour 1930 (4822km)

July 2–July 27, Paris–Paris

1. André Leducq (FRA)	👕	172-12-16
2. Learco Guerra (ITA)		+14-13
3. Antonin Magne (FRA)		+16-03

Le Tour 1931 (5091km)

June 30–July 26, Paris–Paris

1. Antonin Magne (FRA)	👕	177-10-03
2. Joseph Demuysère (BEL)		+12-56
3. Antonio Pesenti (ITA)		+22-51

Le Tour 1932 (4479km)

July 6–July 31, Paris–Paris

1. André Leducq (FRA)	👕	154-11-49
2. Kurt Stoepel (GER)		+24-01
3. Francesco Camusso (ITA)		+26-21

Le Tour 1933 (4395km)

June 27–July 23, Paris–Paris

1. Georges Speicher (FRA)	👕	147-51-37
2. Learco Guerra (ITA)		+4-01
3. Giuseppe Martano (ITA)		+5-08
KoM: Vicente Trueba (SPA)		126 PTS

Le Tour 1934 (4470km)

July 3–July 29, Paris–Paris

1. Antonin Magne (FRA)	👕	147-13-58
2. Giuseppe Martano (ITA)		+27-31
3. Roger Lapébie (FRA)		+52-15
KoM: René Vietto (FRA)		111 PTS

Le Tour 1935 (4338km)

July 4–July 28, Paris–Paris

1. Romain Maes (BEL)	👕	141-32-00
2. Ambrogio Morelli (ITA)		+17-52
3. Félicien Vervaecke (BEL)		+24-06
KoM: Félicien Vervaecke (BEL)		118 PTS

Le Tour 1936 (4418km)

July 7–August 2, Paris–Paris

1. Sylvère Maes (BEL)	👕	142-47-32
2. Antonin Magne (FRA)		+26-55
3. Félicien Vervaecke (BEL)		+27-53
KoM: Julian Berrendero (SPA)		132 PTS

Le Tour 1937 (4415km)

June 30–July 25, Paris–Paris

1. Roger Lapébie (FRA)	👕	138-58-31
2. Mario Vicini (ITA)		+7-17
3. Leo Amberg (SWI)		+26-13
KoM: Félicien Vervaecke (BEL)		114 PTS

Le Tour 1938 (4687km)

July 5–July 31, Paris–Paris

1. Gino Bartali (ITA)	👕	148-29-12
2. Félicien Vervaecke (BEL)		+18-27
3. Victor Cosson (FRA)		+29-26
KoM: Gino Bartali (ITA)		108 PTS

Le Tour 1939 (4224km)

July 10–July 30, Paris–Paris

1. Sylvère Maes (BEL)	👕	132-03-17
2. René Vietto (FRA)		+30-38
3. Lucien Vlaemynck (BEL)		+32-08
KoM: Sylvère Maes (BEL)		85 PTS

Le Tour 1947 (4640km)

June 25–July 20, Paris–Paris

1. Jean Robic (FRA)	👕	148-11-25
2. Ed Fachleitner (FRA)		+3-58
3. Pierre Brambilla (ITA)		+10-07
KoM: Pierre Brambilla (ITA)		98 PTS

Le Tour 1948 (4922km)

June 30–July 25, Paris–Paris

1. Gino Bartali (ITA)	👕	147-10-36
2. Brik Schotte (BEL)		+26-16
3. Guy Lapébie (FRA)		+28-48
KoM: Gino Bartali (ITA)		62 PTS

Le Tour 1949 (4808km)

June 30–July 24, Paris–Paris

1. Fausto Coppi (ITA)	👕	149-40-49
2. Gino Bartali (ITA)		+10-55
3. Jacques Marinelli (FRA)		+25-13
KoM: Fausto Coppi (ITA)		81 PTS

Le Tour 1950 (4773km)

July 13–August 7, Paris–Paris

1. Ferdi Kubler (SWI)	👕	145-36-56
2. Constant "Stan" Ockers (BEL)		+9-30
3. Louison Bobet (FRA)		+22-19
KoM: Louison Bobet (FRA)		58 PTS

Le Tour 1951 (4690km)

July 4–July 29, Paris–Paris

1. Hugo Koblet (SWI)	👕	142-20-14
2. Raphaël Geminiani (FRA)		+22-00
3. Lucien Lazarides (FRA)		+24-16
KoM: Raphaël Geminiani (FRA)		66 PTS

Le Tour 1952 (4898km)

June 25–July 19, Brest–Paris

1. Fausto Coppi (ITA)	👕	151-57-20
2. Constant "Stan" Ockers (BEL)		+28-27
3. Bernardo Ruiz (SPA)		+34-38
KoM: Fausto Coppi (ITA)		92 PTS

Le Tour 1953 (4476km)

July 3–July 26, Strasbourg–Paris

1. Louison Bobet (FRA)	👕	129-23-25
2. Jean Malléjac (FRA)		+14-18
3. Giancarlo Astrua (ITA)		+15-01S
PTS: Fritz Schaer (SWI)	👕	271 PTS
KoM: Jésus Lorono (SPA)		54 PTS

Le Tour 1954 (4656km)

July 8–August 1, Amsterdam–Paris

1. Louison Bobet (FRA)	👕	140-06-05
2. Ferdi Kubler (SWI)		+15-49
3. Fritz Schaer (SWI)		+21-46
PTS: Ferdi Kubler (SWI)	👕	215 PTS
KoM: Federico Bahamontès (SPA)		95 PTS

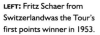

LEFT: Fritz Schaer from Switzerlandwas the Tour's first points winner in 1953.

Le Tour 1955 (4495km)

July 7–July 30, Le Havre–Paris

1. Louison Bobet (FRA)	👕	130-29-26
2. Jean Brankart (BEL)		+4-53
3. Charly Gaul (LUX)		+11-30
PTS: Constant "Stan" Ockers (BEL)	👕	322 PTS
KoM: Charly Gaul (LUX)		84 PTS

Le Tour 1956 (4498km)

July 5–July 28, Reims–Paris

1. Roger Walkowiak (FRA)	👕	124-01-16
2. Gilbert Bauvin (FRA)		+1-25
3. Jan Adriaenssens (BEL)		+3-44
PTS: Constant "Stan" Ockers (BEL)	👕	280 PTS
KoM: Charly Gaul (LUX)		71 PTS

LEFT: Eddy Merckx was back in the yellow jersey after stage six of the 1969 Tour and the Belgian never relinquished it on his way to recording the first of his five Tour wins between 1969 and 1974.

Le Tour 1957 (4665km)

27 June–July 20, Nantes–Paris

1. Jacques Anquetil (FRA)	👕	135-44-42
2. Marc Janssens (BEL)		+14-56
3. Adolf Christian (AUT)		+17-20
PTS: Jean Forestier (FRA)	👕	301 PTS
KoM: Gastone Nencini (ITA)		44 PTS

Le Tour 1958 (4319km)

June 26–July 19, Brussels–Paris

1. Charly Gaul (LUX)	👕	116-59-05
2. Vito Favero (ITA)		+3-10
3. Raphaël Geminiani (FRA)		+3-41
PTS: Jean Graczyk (FRA)	👕	347 PTS
KoM: Federico Bahamontès (SPA)		79 PTS

Le Tour 1959 (4391km)

June 25–July 18, Mulhouse–Paris

1. Federico Bahamontès (SPA)	👕	123-46-45
2. Henri Anglade (FRA)		+4-01
3. Jacques Anquetil (FRA)		+5-05
PTS: André Darrigade (FRA)	👕	613 PTS
KoM: Federico Bahamontès (SPA)		73 PTS

Le Tour 1960 (4173km)

June 26–July 17, Lille–Paris

1. Gastone Nencini (ITA)	👕	112-08-42
2. Graziano Battistini (ITA)		+5-02
3. Jan Adriaenssens (BEL)		+10-24
PTS: Jean Graczyk (FRA)	👕	74 PTS
KoM: Imerio Massignan (ITA)		56 PTS

Le Tour 1961 (4397km)

June 25–July 16, Rouen–Paris

1. Jacques Anquetil (FRA)	👕	122-01-33
2. Guido Carlesi (ITA)		+12-14
3. Charly Gaul (LUX)		+12-16
PTS: André Darrigade (FRA)	👕	174 PTS
KoM: Imerio Massignan (ITA)		56 PTS

Le Tour 1962 (4274km)

June 24–July 15, Nancy–Paris

1. Jacques Anquetil (FRA)	👕	114-31-54
2. Jef Planckaert (BEL)		+4-59
3. Raymond Poulidor (FRA)		+10-24
PTS: Rudi Altig (GER)	👕	173 PTS
KoM: Federico Bahamontès (SPA)		137 PTS

Le Tour 1963 (4137km)

June 23–July 14, Nogent, Paris–Paris

1. Jacques Anquetil (FRA)	👕	113-30-05
2. Fedrico Bahamontès (SPA)		+3-35
3. José Perez-Frances (SPA)		+10-14
PTS: Rik Van Looy (BEL)	👕	275 PTS
KoM: Federico Bahamontès (SPA)		147 PTS

Le Tour 1964 (4504km)

June 22–July 12, Rennes–Paris

1. Jacques Anquetil (FRA)	👕	127-09-44
2. Raymond Poulidor (FRA)		+55SECS
3. Federico Bahamontès (SPA)		+4-44
PTS: Jan Janssen (HOL)	👕	208 PTS
KoM: Federico Bahamontès (SPA)		173 PTS

Le Tour 1965 (4177km)

June 22–July 14, Cologne–Paris

1. Felice Gimondi (ITA)	👕	116-42-06
2. Raymond Poulidor (FRA)		+2-40
3. Gianni Motta (ITA)		+9-18
PTS: Jan Janssen (HOL)	👕	144 PTS
KoM: Julio Jiminez (SPA)		133 PTS

Le Tour 1966 (4322km)

June 21–July 14, Nancy–Paris

1. Lucien Aimar (FRA)	👕	117-34-21
2. Jan Janssen (HOL)		+1-07
3. Raymond Poulidor (FRA)		+2-02
PTS: Willy Planckaert (BEL)	👕	211 PTS
KoM: Julio Jimenez (SPA)		123 PTS

Le Tour 1967 (4758km)

June 29–July 23, Angers–Paris

1. Roger Pingeon (FRA)	👕	136-53-50
2. Julio Jiminez (SPA)		+3-40
3. Franco Balmamion (ITA)		+7-23
PTS: Jan Janssen (HOL)	👕	154 PTS
KoM: Julio Jiminez (SPA)		122 PTS

Le Tour 1968 (4492km)

June 27–July 21, Vittel–Paris

1. Jan Janssen (HOL)	👕	133-49-32
2. Herman Van Springel (BEL)		+38 SECS
3. Ferdinand Bracke (BEL)		+3-03
PTS: Franco Bitossi (ITA)	👕	241 PTS
KoM: Aurelio Gonzales (SPA)		98 PTS

Le Tour 1969 (4117km)

June 28–July 20, Roubaix–Paris

1. Eddy Merckx (BEL)	👕	116-16-02
2. Roger Pingeon (FRA)		+17-54
3. Raymond Poulidor (FRA)		+22-13
PTS: Eddy Merckx (BEL)	👕	244 PTS
KoM: Eddy Merckx (BEL)		155 PTS

Le Tour 1970 (4254km)

June 27–July 19, Limoges–Paris

1. Eddy Merckx (BEL)	👕	119-31-49
2. Joop Zoetemelk (HOL)		+12-41
3. Gösta Pettersson (SWE)		+15-54
PTS: Walter Godefroot (BEL)	👕	212 PTS
KoM: Eddy Merckx (BEL)		128 PTS

Le Tour 1971 (3608km)

June 26–July 18, Mulhouse–Paris

1. Eddy Merckx (BEL)	👕	96-45-14
2. Joop Zoetemelk (HOL)		+9-51
3. Lucien Van Impe (BEL)		+11-06
PTS: Eddy Merckx (BEL)	👕	202 PTS
KoM: Lucien Van Impe (BEL)		228 PTS

166

LEFT: Best climber Lucien Van Impe (polka dot jersey) and eventual overall winner Bernard Thévenet battle up the mountain towards the Puy de Dôme in the 1975 Tour.

Le Tour 1972 (3846km)

July 1–July 23, Angers–Paris

1. Eddy Merckx (BEL)		108-17-18
2. Felice Gimondi (ITA)		+10-41
3. Raymond Poulidor (FRA)		+11-34
PTS: Eddy Merckx (BEL)		196 PTS
KoM: Lucien Van Impe (BEL)		229 PTS

Le Tour 1973 (4090km)

June 30–July 22, La Hay, Scheveningen–Paris

1. Luis Ocana (SPA)		122-25-34
2. Bernard Thévenet (FRA)		+15-49
3. José Manuel Fuente (SPA)		+17-15
PTS: Herman Van Springel (BEL)		187 PTS
KoM: Pedro Torrès (SPA)		225 PTS

Le Tour 1974 (4098km)

June 27–July 21, Brest–Paris

1. Eddy Merckx (BEL)		116-16-58
2. Raymond Poulidor (FRA)		+8-04
3. Vicente Lopez-Carril (SPA)		+8-09
PTS: Patrick Sercu (BEL)		283 PTS
KoM: Domingo Perurena (SPA)		161 PTS

Le Tour 1975 (3999km)

June 26–July 20, Charleroi–Paris

1. Bernard Thévenet (FRA)		114-35-31
2. Eddy Merckx (BEL)		+2-47
3. Lucien Van Impe (BEL)		+5-01
PTS: Rik Van Linden (BEL)		342 PTS
KoM: Lucien Van Impe (BEL)		285 PTS

Le Tour 1976 (4016km)

June 24–July 18, Saint-Jean-de-Monts–Paris

1. Lucien Van Impe (BEL)		116-22-23
2. Joop Zoetemelk (HOL)		+4-14
3. Raymond Poulidor (FRA)		+12-08
PTS: Freddy Maertens (BEL)		293 PTS
KoM: Giancarlo Bellini (ITA)		170 PTS

Le Tour 1977 (4092km)

June 20–July 24, Fleurance–Paris

1. Bernard Thévenet (FRA)		115-38-30
2. Hennie Kuiper (HOL)		+48SEC
3. Lucien Van Impe (BEL)		+3-32
PTS: Jacques Esclassan (FRA)		236 PTS
KoM: Lucien Van Impe (BEL)		244 PTS

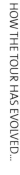

RIGHT: Bernard Hinault, en route to his fourth Tour victory in 1982, is flanked by a pair of Dutchmen, eventual second overall Joop Zoetemelk (left) and climber Peter Winnen on stage 16 to L'Alpe d'Huez.

Le Tour 1978 (3914km)

June 29–July 23, Leiden–Paris

1. Bernard Hinault (FRA)	👕	108-18-00
2. Joop Zoetemelk (HOL)		+3-56
3. Joaqim Agostinho (POR)		+6-54
PTS: Freddy Maertens (BEL)	👕	242 PTS
KoM: Mariano Martinez (SPA)	👕	187 PTS

Le Tour 1979 (3720km)

June 27–July 22, Fleurance–Paris

1. Bernard Hinault (FRA)	👕	103-6-50
2. Joop Zoetemelk (HOL)		+3-07
3. Joaquim Agostinho (POR)		+26-53
PTS: Bernard Hinault (FRA)	👕	253 PTS
KoM: Giovanni Battaglin (ITA)	👕	239 PTS

Le Tour 1980 (3946km)

June 26–July 21, Frankfurt–Paris

1. Joop Zoetemelk (HOL)	👕	109-19-14
2. Hennie Kuiper (HOL)		+6-55
3. Raymond Martin (FRA)		+7-56
PTS: Rudy Pevenage (BEL)	👕	194 PTS
KoM: Raymond Martin (FRA)	👕	210 PTS

Le Tour 1981 (3757km)

June 25–July 19, Nice–Paris

1. Bernard Hinault (FRA)	👕	96-19-38
2. Lucien Van Impe (BEL)		+14-34
3. Robert Alban (FRA)		+17-04
PTS: Freddy Maertens (BEL)	👕	393 PTS
KoM: Lucien Van Impe (BEL)	👕	277 PTS

Le Tour 1982 (3512km)

July 2–July 25, Basle–Paris

1. Bernard Hinault (FRA)	👕	92-08-46
2. Joop Zoetemelk (HOL)		+6-21
3. Johan Vandevelde (HOL)		+8-59
PTS: Sean Kelly (IRE)	👕	429 PTS
KoM: Bernard Vallet (FRA)	👕	273 PTS

Le Tour 1983 (3962km)

July 1–July 24, Fontenay-sous-Bois–Paris

1. Laurent Fignon (FRA)	👕	105-07-52
2. Angel Arroyo (SPA)		+4-04
3. Peter Winnen (HOL)		+4-09
PTS: Sean Kelly (IRE)	👕	330 PTS
KoM: Lucien Van Impe (BEL)	👕	272 PTS

Le Tour 1984 (4021km)

June 29–July 22, Montreuil-sous-Bois–Paris

1. Laurent Fignon (FRA)		112-03-40
2. Bernard Hinault (FRA)		+10-32
3. Greg Lemond (USA)		+11-46
PTS: Frank Hoste (BEL)		322 PTS
KoM: Robert Millar (GBR)		284 PTS

Le Tour 1985 (4127km)

June 28–July 21, Plumelec–Paris

1. Bernard Hinault (FRA)		113-24-23
2. Greg Lemond (USA)		+1-42
3. Stephen Roche (IRE)		+4-29
PTS: Sean Kelly (IRE)		434 PTS
KoM: Luis "Lucho" Herrera (COL)		440 PTS

Le Tour 1986 (4083km)

July 4–July 27, Boulogne-Billancourt–Paris

1. Greg Lemond (USA)		110-35-19
2. Bernard Hinault (FRA)		+3-10
3. Urs Zimmermann (SWI)		+10-54
PTS: Eric Vanderaerden (BEL)		277 PTS
KoM: Bernard Hinault (FRA)		351 PTS

Le Tour 1987 (4231km)

July 1–July 26, West Berlin–Paris

1. Stephen Roche (IRE)		115-27-42
2. Pedro Delgado (SPA)		+40SEC
3. Jean-François Bernard (FRA)		+2-13
PTS: Jean-Paul Van Poppel (HOL)		263 PTS
KoM: Luis "Lucho" Herrera (COL)		452 PTS

Le Tour 1988 (3282km)

July 4–July 24, La Baule–Paris

1. Pedro Delgado (SPA)		84-27-53
2. Steve Rooks (HOL)		+7-13
3. Fabio Parra (COL)		+9-58
PTS: Eddy Planckaert (BEL)		278 PTS
KoM: Steve Rooks (HOL)		326 PTS

Le Tour 1989 (3285km)

July 1–July 23, Luxembourg–Paris

1. Greg Lemond (USA)		87-38-35
2. Laurent Fignon (FRA)		+8SEC
3. Pedro Delgado (SPA)		+3-34
PTS: Sean Kelly (IRE)		277 PTS
KoM: Gert Theunisse (HOL)		441 PTS

Le Tour 1990 (3449km)

June 30–July 22, Futuroscope–Paris

1. Greg Lemond (USA)		90-43-20
2. Claudio Chiappucci (ITA)		+2-16
3. Erik Breukink (HOL)		+2-29
PTS: Olaf Ludwig (GER)		256 PTS
KoM: Thierry Claveyrolat (FRA)		321 PTS

Le Tour 1991 (3914km)

July 6–July 28, Lyon–Paris

1. Miguel Indurain (SPA)		101-01-20
2. Gianni Bugno (ITA)		+3-36
3. Claudio Chiappucci (ITA)		+5-56
PTS: Djamolidine Abdoujaparov (UZB)		316PTS
KoM: Claudio Chiappucci (ITA)		312 PTS

Le Tour 1992 (3983km)

July 4–July 26, San Sébastian–Paris

1. Miguel Indurain (SPA)		100-49-30
2. Claudio Chiappucci (ITA)		+4-35
3. Gianni Bugno (ITA)		+10-49
PTS: Laurent Jalabert (FRA)		293 PTS
KoM: Claudio Chiappucci (ITA)		410 PTS

Le Tour 1993 (3714km)

July 3–July 25, Le Puy de Fou–Paris

1. Miguel Indurain (SPA)		95-57-09
2. Tony Rominger (SWI)		+4-59
3. Zenon Jaskula (POL)		+5-48
PTS: Djamolidine Abdoujaparov (UZB)		298PTS
KoM: Tony Rominger (SWI)		449 PTS

Le Tour 1994 (3978km)

July 2–July 24, Lille–Paris

1. Miguel Indurain (SPA)		103-38-38
2. Piotr Ugrumov (LAT)		+5-39
3. Marco Pantani (ITA)		+7-19
PTS: Djamolidine Abdoujaparov (UZB)		322PTS
KoM: Richard Virenque (FRA)		392 PTS

Le Tour 1995 (3653km)

July 1–July 23, Saint Brieuc–Paris

1. Miguel Indurain (SPA)		92-44-59
2. Alex Zülle (SWI)		+4-35
3. Bjarne Riis (DEN)		+6-47
PTS: Laurent Jalabert (FRA)		333 PTS
KoM: Richard Virenque (FRA)		438 PTS

Le Tour 1996 (3907km)

June 29–July 21, 's-Hertogenbosch–Paris

1. Bjarne Riis (DEN)		95-57-16
2. Jan Ullrich (GER)		+1-41
3. Richard Virenque (FRA)		+4-37
PTS: Erik Zabel (GER)		335 PTS
KoM: Richard Virenque (FRA)		383 PTS

Le Tour 1997 (3950km)

July 5–July 27, Rouen–Paris

1. Jan Ullrich (GER)		100-30-35
2. Richard Virenque (FRA)		+9-09
3. Marco Pantani (ITA)		+14-03
PTS: Erik Zabel (GER)		320 PTS
KoM: Richard Virenque (FRA)		579 PTS

Le Tour 1998 (3875km)

July 11–August 2, Dublin–Paris

1. Marco Pantani (ITA)		92-49-46
2. Jan Ullrich (GER)		+3-21
3. Bobby Julich (USA)		+4-08
PTS: Erik Zabel (GER)		327 PTS
KoM: Christophe Rinero (FRA)		200 PTS

Le Tour 1999* (3686km)

July 3–July 25, Le Puy de Fou–Paris

1. Lance Armstrong (USA)		91-32-16
2. Alex Zülle (SWI)		+7-37
3. Fernardo Escartin (SPA)		+10-26
PTS: Erik Zabel (GER)		323 PTS
KoM: Richard Virenque (FRA)		279 PTS

Le Tour 2000* (3630km)

July 1–July 23, Futuroscope–Paris

1. Lance Armstrong (USA)		92-33-08
2. Jan Ullrich (GER)		+6-02
3. Joseba Beloki (SPA)		+10-04
PTS: Erik Zabel (GER)		321 PTS
KoM: Santiago Botero (COL)		347 PTS

Le Tour 2001* (3446km)

July 7–July 29, Dunkirk–Paris

1. Lance Armstrong (USA)		86-17-28
2. Jan Ullrich (GER)		+6-44
3. Joseba Beloki (SPA)		+9-05
PTS: Erik Zabel (GER)		252 PTS
KoM: Laurent Jalabert (FRA)		258 PTS

Le Tour 2002* (3282km)

July 7–July 29, Luxembourg–Paris

1. Lance Armstrong (USA)		82-05-12
2. Joseba Beloki (SPA)		+7-17
3. Raimondas Rumsas (LIT)		+8-17
PTS: Robbie McEwen (AUS)		280 PTS
KoM: Laurent Jalabert (FRA)		262 PTS

Le Tour 2003* (3350km)

July 5–July 27, Paris–Paris

1. Lance Armstrong (USA)		83-41-12
2. Jan Ullrich (GER)		+1-01
3. Alexandre Vinokourov (KAZ)		+4-14
PTS: Baden Cooke (AUS)		216 PTS
KoM: Richard Virenque (FRA)		324 PTS

Le Tour 2004* (3390km)

July 3–July 25, Liege–Paris

1. Lance Armstrong (USA)		83-36-02
2. Andreas Kloden (GER)		+6-19
3. Ivan Basso (ITA)		+6-40
PTS: Robbie McEwen (AUS)		272 PTS
KoM: Richard Virenque (FRA)		226 PTS

LEFT: Wearing the polka dot jersey of the leading climber, Richard Virenque celebrates winning stage 14, from Le Bourg-d'Oisans to Courchevel, in the 1997 Tour.

170

Le Tour 2005* (3607km)

July 2–24, Fromentine–Paris

1. Lance Armstrong (USA)	👕	86-15-02
2. Ivan Basso (ITA)		+4-40
3. Jan Ullrich (GER)		+6-21
PTS: Thor Hushovd (NOR)	👕	194 PTS
KoM: Michael Rasmussen (DEN)	👕	185 PTS

Le Tour 2006** (3657km)

July 1–July 23, Strasbourg–Paris

1. Floyd Landis (USA)	👕	89-38-39
2. Oscar Pereiro (SPA)		+57SEC
3. Andreas Klöden (GER)		+1-29
PTS: Robbie McEwen (AUS)	👕	288 PTS
KoM: Michael Rasmussen (DEN)	👕	166 PTS

Le Tour 2007 (3547km)

July 7–July 29, London–Paris

1. Alberto Contador (SPA)	👕	91-00-26
2. Cadel Evans (AUS)		+23SEC
3. Levi Leipheimer (USA)		+31SEC
PTS: Tom Boonen (BEL)	👕	256 PTS
KoM: Mauricio Soler (COL)	👕	206 PTS

Le Tour 2008 (3554km)

July 5–July 27, Brest–Paris

1. Carlos Sastre (SPA)	👕	87-52-52
2. Cadel Evans (AUS)		+58SEC
3. Bernard Kohl (AUT)		+1-13
PTS: Oscar Freire (SPA)	👕	270 PTS
KoM: Bernard Kohl (AUT)	👕	128 PTS

Le Tour 2009 (3459.5km)

July 4–July 26, Monaco–Paris

1. Alberto Contador (SPA)	👕	81-46-17
2. Andy Schleck (LUX)		+4-11
3. Lance Armstrong (USA)		+5-24
PTS: Thor Hushovd (NOR)	👕	260 PTS
KoM: Franco Pellizotti (ITA)	👕	210 PTS

Le Tour 2010*** (3642km)

July 3–July 25, Rotterdam–Paris

1. Alberto Contador (SPA)	👕	91-58-48
2. Andy Schleck (LUX)		+39SEC
3. Denis Menchov (RUS)		+2-01
PTS: Alessandro Petacchi (ITA)	👕	243 PTS
KoM: Anthony Charteau (FRA)	👕	143 PTS

Le Tour 2011 (3430km)

July 2–July 24,
Passage du Gois La Barre-de-Monts–Paris

1. Cadel Evans (AUS)	👕	86-12-22
2. Andy Schleck (LUX)		+1-34
3. Frank Schleck (LUX)		+2-30
PTS: Mark Cavendish (GBR)	👕	334PTS
KoM: Samuel Sanchez (SPA)	👕	108PTS

Le Tour 2012 (3497km)

June 30–July 22, Liège–Paris

1. Bradley Wiggins (GBR)	👕	87-34-47
2. Chris Froome (GBR)		+3-21
3. Vincenzo Nibali (ITA)		+6-19
PTS: Peter Sagan (SLO)	👕	421PTS
KoM: Thomas Voeckler (FRA)	👕	135PTS

Le Tour 2013 (3404km)

June 29–July 21, Porto Vecchio–Paris

1. Chris Froome (GBR)	👕	83-56-40
2. Naira Quintana (COL)		+4-20
3. Joaquim Rodriguez (SPA)		+5-04
PTS: Peter Sagan (SLO)	👕	409PTS
KoM: Nairo Quintana (COL)	👕	147PTS

Le Tour 2014 (3660km)

July 5–July 27, Leeds–Paris

1. Vincenzo Nibali (ITA)	👕	89-59-06
2. Jean-Christophe Péraud (FRA)		+7-39
3. Thibaut Pinot (FRA)		+8-15
PTS: Peter Sagan (SLO)	👕	431PTS
KOM: Rafal Majka (POL)	👕	181PTS

Le Tour 2015 (3360km)

July –July 26, Utrecht–Paris

1. Chris Froome (GBR)	👕	84-46-14
2. Nairo Quintana (COL)		+1-12
3. Alejandro Valverde (SPA)		+5-25
PTS: Peter Sagan (SLO)	👕	432PTS
KOM: Chris Froome (GBR)	👕	119PTS

Le Tour 2016 (3529km)

July 2–July 24, Mont St Michel–Paris

1. Chris Froome (GBR)	👕	89-04-48
2. Romain Bardet (FRA)		+4-05
3. Nairo Quintana (COL)		+4-21
PTS: Peter Sagan (SLO)	👕	470PTS
KOM: Rafal Majka (POL)	👕	209PTS

Le Tour 2017 (3540km)

July 1–July 23 Dusseldorf–Paris

1. Chris Froome (GBR)	👕	86-20-55
2. Rigoberto Uran (COL)		+54SEC
3. Romain Bardet (FRA)		+2-20
PTS: Michael Matthews (AUS)	👕	370PTS
KOM: Warren Barguil (FRA)	👕	169PTS

Le Tour 2018 (3,351km)

July 7–July 29 Noirmoutier-en-l'Ile–Paris

1. Geraint Thomas (GBR)	👕	83-17-13
2. Tom Dumoulin (HOL)		+1-51
3. Chris Froome (GBR)		+2-24
PTS: Peter Sagan (SLO)	👕	477PTS
KOM: Julian Alaphilippe (FRA)	👕	170PTS

Le Tour 2019 (3,366km)

July 6–July 28 Brussels–Paris

1. Egan Bernal (COL)	👕	82-57-00
2. Geraint Thomas (GBR)		+1-11
3. Steven Kruijswijk (NED)		+1-31
PTS: Peter Sagan (SLO)	👕	316PTS
KOM: Romain Bardet (FRA)	👕	86PTS

Le Tour 2020 (3,484km)

August 29–September 20 Nice–Paris

1. Tadej Pogacar (SLO)	👕	87-20-05
2. Primoz Roglic (SLO)		+59SEC
3. Richie Porte (AUS)		+3-30
PTS: Sam Bennett (IRE)	👕	380PTS
KOM: Tadej Pogacar (SLO)	👕	82PTS

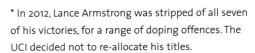

* In 2012, Lance Armstrong was stripped of all seven of his victories, for a range of doping offences. The UCI decided not to re-allocate his titles.

** Following a positive dope test during the 2006 Tour, Floyd Landis was stripped of his victory and Oscar Pereiro was named as the winner. Andreas Klöden was promoted to second place and third was Carlos Sastre of Spain at +3-13.

*** Following a positive dope test during the 2010 Tour, Alberto Contador was stripped of his victory and Andy Schleck was named as the winner. Denis Menchov was promoted to second place, and third was Samuel Sanchez of Spain at +3-01.

OPPOSITE: Eventual green jersey winner Peter Sagan edges out Alexander Kristoff to win stage 16 into Bern on the 2016 Tour.

Index

INDEX

172

174

About the authors

SERGE LAGET was seven years old when the 1954 Tour de France visited the Cévennes region of southern France and it enthralled him. Although reading and collecting stories in *L'Equipe* – the newspaper for which he would later write – gave him an insight into Le Tour, nothing quite compared with the image of the squadron of white Peugeot 203s surrounding Louison Bobet and Ferdi Kübler as they rode through the Pradelles hills. His passion grew as time passed but the dream turned into reality when Laget not only met Jean "Apo" Lazaridès, André Darrigade and Raymond Poulidor but also, with mentors such as Pierre Chany, Jacques Augendre and Jacques Goddet, wrote about them in articles and books. He knows how lucky he has been to be involved with the Tour and wants to share his good fortune – the story of the Tour de France is a great one.

LUKE EDWARDES-EVANS, has been a cycling journalist for more than 30 years, working as a reporter for *Cycling Weekly* and editor of *Winning – Bicycle Racing Illustrated*, *Cycle Sport*, *Cycling Active* and *Tour* magazines. He has edited dozens of Tour race guides and, as a fan, has cycled up many of the Tour's legendary mountain passes in the Alps and Pyrenees. He has been privileged to know some of the great English-speaking Tour riders and has a deep appreciation of the dedication and suffering familiar to all Tourmen. His other job is a motorcycle driver working in pro bike racing with a cycling photographer on the back. He was privileged to follow the centenary Tour of 2013 as well as the 2014 and 2017 (with *L'Equipe*) editions. He is quite possibly the only person to have worked on full Tours as both a reporter (1990) and a motorcycle rider!

ANDY MCGRATH is the Editor of *Rouleur Magazine*. His passion for the Tour was piqued as an adolescent when he saw Lance Armstrong fighting Carlos Sastre up La Plagne in the 2002 Tour. He simply had to know more about this big race. A few years, and a lot more knowledge, later, he became a cycling journalist and has gone on to cover several Tours de France, as well as the Tour of Italy and the sport's big one-day Classics. Seeing various facets of the Tour – from a day spent on the publicity caravan to hours in teams cars, press conferences and even suffering up the tough mountains – he appreciates the Tour's generosity, beauty and charm more than ever.

Credits

Editorial Director: Martin Corteel
Project Editor: Ross Hamilton
Project Art Editor: Luke Griffin
Designer: Eliana Holder
Production: Rachel Burgess
Picture Research: Paul Langan

All photographs in this book are courtesy of
© Presse Sports / Offside Sports Photography

Every effort has been made to acknowledge correctly and contact the source and/or copyright holder of each picture and Welbeck Non-Fiction Limited apologises for any unintentional errors or omissions, which will be corrected in future editions of this book.

ABOVE: Press pass for journalist R. Boisserie for the 50th edition of the Tour de France. Although 1963 was the 60th anniversary of the Tour, 11 races were not staged because of the two World Wars (four 1915–18 and seven 1940–46). M Boisserie was permitted to ride in the vehicles which follow the riders.